PRAISE FOR *Made for Goodness:*

"Tutu asks so many essential questions in the first two pages of this book—how to keep faith in people with so much cruelty in view, how to see goodness where others see only injustice and oppression—that one may be forgiven for counting the pages he has left to answer them. Yet Tutu and his daughter do not disappoint. On page after page, with disarming narrative skill, they tell true stories in which both brutality and hopefulness turn out to be as intimate as they are global. If you are still open to being convinced that goodness changes everything—and that you are a creature of agency who can affect the course of creation—then this book is for you. Read it at least twice before you give it to everyone you know. The 'God-pressure' in these pages is palpable, and there is no time to lose."

—Barbara Brown Taylor, author of *Altar in the World*

"I doubt there is anyone on this earth with a deeper sense of God's presence and goodness than Archbishop Tutu. To read his forthright advice is to feel oneself embraced by Providence and surrounded by Love. If you are thirsty for spiritual drink, come to the water of this beautiful book."

—Thomas Cahill, author of *How the Irish Saved Civilization* and *The Gift of the Jews*

"Archbishop Tutu lives and breathes goodness. Even with the incredible trauma and cruelty he endured in South Africa during apartheid and the many atrocities he has witnessed in his life, he still radiates love and happiness. This wonderful new book, *Made for Goodness*, that he has written with his daughter shares how he consistently believes in the goodness within all of us. This book is a great gift to the world and will help all of us celebrate our goodness and oneness."

—Sir Richard Branson, founder and chairman
of the Virgin Group

"Desmond Tutu has walked the talk all his adult life. He gives of himself to individuals and to groups, and in everything he does there is a deep, compelling spirituality. We can all be grateful that together with his daughter Mpho, he has now shared his secrets for why he has so much hope and joy."

—Mary Robinson, former president of Ireland

"Our boss and his daughter remind us here how clearly we are one: I am, because we are. The Tutu family takes us back to that fundamental truth, showing us that at the end of even the very worst day, it's in our DNA to look out for our brothers and sisters."

—Bono, lead singer of U2 and co-founder of
ONE and (RED)

"As the author so clearly and beautifully says in this book, 'anyone can choose to cultivate compassion.' Thank you Archbishop Tutu for helping us all come back home to our true nature, which is inherently good and whole, and touch the peace that is always there for us."

—Thich Nhat Hanh, author of *The Art of Power*
and *Savor*

MADE FOR GOODNESS

MADE FOR GOODNESS

And Why This Makes All the Difference

DESMOND M. TUTU

AND

MPHO A. TUTU

Edited by Douglas C. Abrams

HarperOne

An Imprint of HarperCollins*Publishers*

HarperOne

Bible quotations, unless otherwise noted, are from the New Revised Standard Version of the Bible, copyright © 1989 by the Division of Christian Education of the National Council of Churches of Christ in the U.S.A.

HarperCollins books may be purchased for educational, business, or sales promotional use. For information please write: Special Markets Department, HarperCollins Publishers, 10 East 53rd Street, New York, NY 10022.

HarperCollins Web site: http://www.harpercollins.com
HarperCollins®, ■ ®, and HarperOne™ are
trademarks of HarperCollins Publishers

FIRST EDITION

Library of Congress Cataloging-in-Publication Data is available upon request.

ISBN 978–0–06–170659–2

10 11 12 13 14 RRD (H) 10 9 8 7 6 5 4 3 2 1

To Roro, our children and grandchildren
—DMT

To Joe, Nyaniso, and Onalenna
—MAT

CONTENTS

PREFACE

I speak to audiences across the world, and I often get the same questions: "Why are you so joyful?" "How do you keep your faith in people when you see so much injustice, oppression, and cruelty?" "What makes you so certain that the world is going to get better?"

What these questioners really want to know is, What do I see that they're missing? How do I see the world and my role in it? How do I see God? What is the faith that drives me? What are the spiritual practices that uphold me? What do I see in the heart of humanity and in the sweep of history that confirms my conviction that goodness will triumph?

This book is my answer.

I have written with the help of my youngest daughter, Mpho. Like me, she is a priest in the Anglican Communion. We are both parents, both married, and we share some core beliefs. But each of us has our own unique life experience that we bring to this book.

Our experience, our reading of Scripture, and the people who have been a part of our lives—however briefly—have taught us some important truths that we will share with you in this book. First, we will see that we are all designed for goodness, and when we recognize that truth it makes all the difference in the world. Second, we are perfectly loved with a love that requires nothing of us, so we can stop "being good" and live into the goodness that is our essence. And third, God holds out an invitation to us—an invitation to turn away from the anxious striving that has turned stress into a status symbol. It is an invitation to wholeness that leads to flourishing for all of us.

We also know that God has given us the gift of freedom and that in order for freedom to be real, we must be free to choose right and equally free to choose wrong. With our freedom comes certain hard questions: Where is God when we suffer? Where is God when we fail? Why does God let us sin? And when we do suffer, fail, or sin, how do we find our way home to goodness? How can we rediscover our essence? We will explore these questions together. We will also describe some of the ways we have learned of hearing God's voice offer us comfort, guidance, answers, and acceptance. When we are able to hear God's voice and see with God's eyes, we will be able to see the world as it truly is.

We will explore the truths and address the questions using the stories that have shaped our outlook. Our worldview was forged in the fires of apartheid South Africa and in the course of marriage and parenting, and so we will share many stories from our homes and our history. You will also become familiar with some of our favorite Bible stories. Whether you read the Bible as sacred text or just as good literature, the stories it contains tell us deep and abiding truths about human nature. We return to them again and again in our teaching and preaching and in our private prayer and study.

We invite you to join us on a pilgrimage. Come and see some of the places we have seen. Come and share some of the lessons we have learned. Come and meet some of the people we have known. Walk with us on holy ground. Perhaps you will learn to see yourself through God's eyes and come to know that your whole life is holy ground.

MADE FOR GOODNESS

1

THE DIFFERENCE
GOODNESS MAKES

Impimpi!" ("Informer!")

In the bad old days of apartheid the accusation was deadly. Any black person suspected of collaborating with the hated South African security police risked a grisly death. Here the suspected informer was down on the ground, beaten and bloodied. Tempers in the crowd were already frayed. It was yet another in a long procession of the struggle funerals: Duduza Township, east of Johannesburg, in July 1985. It was thought that police had killed the four young men we had come to bury. And now the crowd had their hands on a man they accused of being a police spy. They were preparing the petrol-filled tire that was to be his fiery "necklace."

Without pausing to think, I waded into the middle of the angry mob. "Do you accept us as your leaders?" I asked. They seemed rather reluctant, mumbling. "If you accept us as your leaders, you have to listen to us and stop what you are doing." As I desperately tried to reason with the crowd a car arrived, and my colleague Bishop Simeon Nkoane was able to spirit the injured man away. It was only afterward, when I saw it on television, that I considered my own peril. I tell this not as a story of my heroism but as an illustration of the violence we can inflict upon one another.

I am no dispassionate observer of the litany of crime and cruelty that assaults us at every turn. For three long years I served as the chairman of South Africa's Truth and Reconciliation Commission, our attempt to cleanse our nation's soul from the evil of apartheid. For days on end I listened to horrific stories of abuse. I cannot tell you how many times my heart broke as I listened to the confessions of perpetrators and the testimony of victims. Indeed, at times I became sick to my stomach at the horror of what I heard.

It is not only what I have heard of human depravity that has made my stomach churn, but also what I have seen. As the president of the All Africa Conference of Churches, I made a pastoral visit to Rwanda in 1995, a year after the genocide. I went to Ntarama, where hundreds of Tutsis had fled to the church for safety. The year 1994 was not the first time that interethnic violence had gripped Rwanda. With each previous eruption of fighting any church became a refuge, a sanctuary from the insanity beyond its walls. In 1994 the Hutu Power movement respected no sanctuary. Tutsi people were slaughtered in churches throughout Rwanda. The Ntarama church was no different. It provided no safety for the people, mostly women and children, who had cowered there. The floor was strewn with a record of the horror that had occurred in that place. Clothing and suitcases were scattered among the bones. The small skulls of children lay shattered on the floor. The new government had not removed the corpses, so the church was like a mortuary, with the bodies lying as they had fallen the year before. The stench was overpowering. Outside the church building was a collection of skulls, some still stuck with machetes and daggers. I tried to pray. I could only weep.

All over the world people have inflicted unspeakable violence on other people. On missions to the Sudan, to Gaza, and to Northern Ireland I have borne witness to some of the viciousness that human beings can unleash on each other.

Brutality can be as intimate as it is global. Our cruelties are played out in the intimacy of our own homes and neighborhoods as much as they are experienced on the world stage. I have shared my daughter Mpho's anguish as she has described some of her experiences in ministry to me. She has worked with rape survivors in South Africa: a fifteen-year-old girl who spent countless nights sleeping in the school bathroom to escape her father's molestation and her mother's rage and impotence. Mpho cared for an eight-year-old girl twice violated by a neighbor. Because the neighbor had threatened to kill her family, the frightened child named someone else as the perpetrator the first time she was molested. It was only after the second assault that she dared to tell the truth. My daughter sat with an eighty-year-old woman brutalized by a stranger. She listened as the doctor who attended the victim struggled to contain her own distress: "The genital lacerations were so ragged and awful, I hardly knew where to begin to sew her up." In Massachusetts, Mpho worked with women of many races and every economic stratum who had fled from domestic violence to homelessness. She has been with wealthy women too ashamed to turn to their friends for support or shelter, and poor women who had nowhere to go. She has provided pastoral counseling to families struggling with the effects of substance abuse: loss of livelihood, loss of self-respect, frayed family ties, and, often, violence.

As married persons, as priests, and as parents we have both encountered the disappointments, failures, and despair that can infect human relationships. Hearing my mother's screams and my father's drunken beatings, I have known that noxious brew of fear and rage that courses through a small boy. Even as adults in our own marriages, we have both known moments when the joy of marriage shrivels in the heat of a bitter argument.

We know all too well the cruelties, hurts, and hatreds that poison life on our planet. But my daughter and I have come together to write this book because we know that the catalogue of injuries that we can and do inflict on one another is not the whole story of humanity, not by a long measure—as I hope you will see and as you no doubt know in your heart. We are indeed made for something more. We are made for goodness.

We are fundamentally good. When you come to think of it, that's who we are at our core. Why else do we get so outraged by wrong? When we hear of any egregious act, we are appalled. Isn't that an incredible assertion about us? Evil and wrong are aberrations. If wrong was the norm, it wouldn't be news. Our newscasts wouldn't lead with the latest acts of murder or mayhem, because they would be ordinary. But murder and mayhem are not the norm. The norm is goodness.

You can see from the people we truly admire that we are attracted to goodness. We do not revere people who are successful. We might envy them and wish that their money were transferred to our bank account. But the people we revere are not necessarily successful; they are something else. They are good.

Many of us would say we revere Mother Teresa. She wasn't macho. She wasn't even successful. In spite of her many years of lauded and dedicated ministry, people still die in poverty in Calcutta. But even after her death, Mother Teresa is admired, respected, and revered. Mahatma Gandhi and Martin Luther King Jr. are similarly revered not for their success, although they had important successes, but because of the shining example of their goodness. In our own time Nelson Mandela commands the same kind of admiration. He walks into any place, and people are transfixed—not because he is mighty and macho, but because he is gracious and good.

You and I, too, are fundamentally good. We are tuned to the key of goodness. This is not to deny evil; it is to face evil squarely. And we can face evil squarely because we know that evil will not have the last word.

Evil cannot have the last word because we are pro-grammed—no, hard-wired—for goodness. Yes, goodness can be enlightened self-interest. Kindness builds goodwill. Generosity invites reciprocation. But even if there were absolutely no material benefit to being kind, you can't coun-terfeit the warm glow that you have inside when you have been kind. You just can't! That glow is something you relish because that's how we've been created. To be hateful and mean is operating against the deepest yearnings that God placed in our hearts. Goodness is not just our impulse. It is our essence.

Recognizing the truth about our goodness matters more now than ever. Our world is shrinking. Modern technology has brought people from the ends of the earth into our living rooms. Our communities have become less homogeneous. People of many cultures, races, religions, and ethnic back-grounds share our neighborhoods and meet on our streets. We can be halfway across the world in less time than it takes to drive halfway across many countries. In the past, conflicts could be contained in one country, one region, one conti-nent. But the push of a button by an anonymous hand can launch a missile that will engulf the world in war.

In the past our survival depended on recognizing and being suspicious of difference. If people were in and of our group, we could assume good intent. If people were not in and of our group, we would be safest to assume evil inten-tions. Vestiges of that belief are retained in our behavior.

Palestinians face Israelis across hopeless barriers of mistrust. Christians shout down Muslims without letting their voices be heard. And we argue endlessly about the efficacy of racial profiling in keeping our communities safe.

What the catalogue of fault lines illustrates is that the atomized homogeneous groups that existed in the past are no longer the truth of our world. Our planet will not survive if we cling to the verities of the past. We must recognize that we are part of one group, one family—the human family. Our survival as a planet depends on it. We are part of one family, and we are fundamentally good.

What difference does goodness make? Goodness changes everything. If we are at core selfish, cruel, heartless creatures, we need to fight these inclinations at every turn and often need strong systems of control to prevent us from revealing our true (and quite ugly) selves. But if we are fundamentally good, we simply need to rediscover this true nature and act accordingly. This insight into our essential goodness has shifted how I interact with other people; it has even shaken how I read the Bible.

Goodness changes the way we see the world, the way we see others, and, most importantly, the way we see ourselves. The way we see ourselves matters. It affects how we treat people. It affects the quality of life for each and all of us. What is the quality of life on our planet? It is nothing more than the sum total of our daily interactions. Each kindness enhances the quality of life. Each cruelty diminishes it.

If we believe that we are fundamentally cruel and selfish, we act accordingly. The targets of our nastiness feel the effects of our malice. And the consequences of our cruelty are evident in our health. Meanness shows on our faces. Churlishness shows up in our bodies as stress and illness. It is also true that when we recognize our fundamental goodness, we act differently. And we feel different. We are happier, healthier. God is pretty smart. It feels good to be good. And we know it! When we attend to our deepest yearnings, our very nature, our life changes forever, and, person by person, so does our world.

We are made for goodness by God, who is goodness itself. We are made for and like God, who is the very essence of goodness. The creation stories in the Hebrew Bible underline these truths about us. These stories do not set out to tell us scientific facts. They set out to tell us governing truths, truths that affect how we live our lives. Whether, like Mpho and me, you read the Bible as sacred text or, if as one who does not share in the Abrahamic faiths, you read it merely as good literature, it offers insight and wisdom distilled from centuries of human experience. And the fundamental point of the creation stories is that we are made by God, for God, like God. But what does this mean?

In the first book of the Bible, the book of Genesis, there are two creation stories. Each tells a particular truth about us. In the first Genesis story God speaks creation into being. Turn with me to these beautiful words. Let us read them for the profound truth they tell rather than for scientific accuracy.

In the beginning when God created the heavens and the earth, the earth was a formless void and darkness covered the face of the deep, while a wind from God swept over the face of the waters. Then God said, "Let there be light"; and there was light. And God saw that the light was good; and God separated the light from the darkness. God called the light Day and the darkness he called Night. And there was evening and there was morning, the first day. (Gen. 1:1–5)

For five days creation is born from the mouth of God with the words, "Let there be. . . ." Light and darkness; the oceans and the heavens; the sky, the seas, and the dry land; vegetation of every kind: trees and seeds, fruit and flowers; the sun, moon, and stars; the sea creatures and the birds of the air; living creatures of every kind: cattle, wild animals, and creeping things—all come into being at God's "Let there be. . . ." Then, on the sixth day, there is a change. The storyteller has to give a signal that something momentous is about to occur: instead of the formula for every other act of creation—"Let there be. . . ."—for this one, God says, "Let us. . . ." It's as though God has to consult. The entire divine court has to be involved in the emergence of this extraordinary creature that is in the image of God, the likeness of God, who is going to be God's representative, the steward of God's creation.

Then God said, "Let us make humankind in our image, according to our likeness; and let them have dominion over the fish of the sea, and over the birds of the air, and over the cattle, and over all the wild animals of the earth, and over every creeping thing that creeps upon the earth."

So God created humankind in his image, in the image of God he created them; male and female he created them. (Gen. 1:26–27)

And when God has completed this act of creation, God sees not that "it was good," as God said at the end of all the other acts of creation. God sees something more. At the end of this sixth day, "God saw everything that he had made, and indeed it was *very* good" (Gen. 1:31). All of it was *very* good, including us; no part of it is inherently evil.

We are very good. How can we believe this when we see the horror and grief we inflict on each other? We can believe it because we know that we are made in the very image and likeness of God. We say this not only as a faith statement or creed. We say this because we have found that it is the best way to express who and what we are. Perhaps you, like most of us, really do not understand the incredible creatures we are. Perhaps you have not taken in what it means to be made in the image of God. We forget. Or we don't really believe it. But we are made in the image of God. It is as though we want to be dwarfs when God wants us to be giants.

We are endowed, like the creator, with this gift of creativity. Anyone who has seen a dancer in motion or an artist at work, anyone who has enjoyed the skill of a good cook or watched a child build a sandcastle or make a mud pie knows that human creativity is inherent.

We may apply our creativity to good ends or ill. Human artistry can be used to decorate a home or forge a banknote. Human resourcefulness can combine the chemicals to purify a well or poison a watercourse. The beautiful gardens at the Palace of Versailles in France and at Mount Vernon in Virginia were the fruit of human inventiveness. The minefields that still kill and maim in Angola and Cambodia were also planned and planted by human beings.

In our creativity we are like God. We are also like God in our freedom. God is self-constrained in relationship to us. God leaves us free to choose how we apply our gifts and talents. Like a good parent, God renders God's-self powerfully powerless in the face of our choices. When we see the pride shining in a mother's eyes as her little darling squeals out his first clarinet recital, we can imagine the face of God as God surveys our successes. When we watch the pained calm of a parent listening to a report of his child's misdeeds, we can imagine the anguished eyes of God as God sees us stumble, fall, and fail. In all the diverse expressions of humanity we are made like God.

We are made not only like God but also for God. Planted in the center of our being is a longing for the holy. "Don't you know," the Christian letter writer Saint Paul asks, "that you are a temple of the Holy Spirit?" People of faith treat a temple with the utmost respect and reverence. Even for those of no faith there are places that are accorded the status of temples; for some it might be their house or garden, into which they pour all of their effort and love. My wife, Leah, hates housework but will joyfully spend endless hours tending her garden. Each of our homes has been lovely and well maintained, but our gardens have always been true spiritual oases, places for the soul to be refreshed. For some people it might be an office or workshop that is accorded the status of temple: it is maintained with a kind of reverence.

We are temples of the Holy Spirit. Not just our bodies but our very selves, the essence of our being, is the place in which the Spirit resides. The Spirit within us calls out to God to find its place and its home. Saint Augustine says, "You have made us for yourself, O Lord, and our hearts are restless until they find their rest in you."

Being made for God means, for us, that anything less than God will not suffice. We are hungry for God, but we don't always know that it is God that we crave. Often we are like the woman who stands at the open refrigerator door at three o'clock in the morning knowing that she is hungry for something but not knowing what it is that she needs, so she shuts the mouth of her hunger with something that merely stupefies but does not satisfy. We stand around feeling a vague dissatisfaction and having no idea of what it is that we actually want. So we shut the mouth of our desire for God with busyness, or with things—gadgets, gizmos, trinkets, and treasures—and emerge at the other end recognizing that what we have is not what we need.

We yearn for God, yet we feel lost on the way to our own hearts. We want to live lives of goodness. We long for a teacher and adviser close enough to speak the words of wisdom to guide us. Who is this teacher, this adviser? Many can help us along the way, but in the end it is only God whose advice we really need to hear. But how can we reach God? How can we hear what God has to say to us? God may seem distant and inaccessible. Sometimes we stop hearing the voice of God in our lives. And sometimes, though we hear God's voice, God seems not to speak our language.

In this book we will share how we have learned to talk with God. More importantly, we will tell you how we have heard God speak to us. We will offer some ways you can tune yourself to God's frequency, some ways to understand God's language, ways to listen and hear God's words of guidance for your own life. Ultimately, what stirs us most deeply is what is life giving. What is soul stirring, what is life giving, is of God. We are made for God, who is the giver of life. We are made by God, who holds us in life.

We are animated and held in life by the very breath of God. It is God's breath that sustains us. Let us turn again to the book of Genesis, this time to the second creation story. As the mother of a young child for whom puddles and mud are current wonders, Mpho is always captivated by the image in the second creation story. In that narrative we can almost see God playing in the dirt and creating from the dust the earth being, Adam. And we watch God blowing the breath of life, God's own breath, into this first human.

In the day that the Lord God made the earth and the heavens, when no plant of the field was yet in the earth and no herb of the field had yet sprung up—for the Lord God had not caused it to rain upon the earth, and there was no one to till the ground; but a stream would rise from the earth, and water the whole face of the ground—then the Lord God formed man from the dust of the ground, and breathed into his nostrils the breath of life; and the man became a living being. (Gen. 2:4–7)

We who are human are being kept in being by the very breath of God from moment to moment. Each moment is a choice of God. If God stopped, even for the fraction of a second, from upholding us, from breathing God's breath into us, we would disintegrate. Which is an incredible statement about God; because God does that even for the ones that we call bad people, evil people. God is as intimate with them as God is intimate with the most saintly. There is not a single person that God gives up on, because God knows that we are made to be like God, who is goodness itself.

This is not only a faith claim. It is a scientific fact. Science testifies that goodness is a survival strategy. God created us to depend on each other for our very lives. As primatologist Frans de Waal explains, "We belong to the category of animals known among zoologists as 'obligatorily gregarious,' meaning that we have no option but to stick together. This is why fear of ostracism lurks in the corners of every human mind: being expelled is the worst thing that can befall us. It was so in biblical times, and it remains so today. Evolution has instilled a need to belong and to feel accepted. We are social to our core."

Early studies of human survival have noted the "fight or flight" stress response. Newer research has observed that not everyone responds to stress in the same way: instead of fight or flight, some adopt a "tend and befriend" response. By caring for the young and banding together for protection and support, we have ensured the survival of the species. This pattern of relationship building not only ensures physical survival but also contributes to psychic well-being. Those who have been involved in the more nurturing aspects of child rearing can testify to the psychic satisfaction of rocking a baby to sleep. Mpho and I both know the simple joy of being able to heal a hurt with a kiss and banish midnight monsters with a cuddle. Caring for the weak and vulnerable has health benefits for the caregiver as well as for the recipient of the attention. Elder-care settings have demonstrated the physical and psychological benefits to seniors of caring for small animals. Having a pet to tend can soothe anxious children.

Ubuntu is the Xhosa word used to describe the "tend and befriend" survival behavior. *Ubuntu* recognizes that human beings need each other for survival and well-being. A person is a person only through other persons, we say. We must care for one another in order to thrive.

The impulse to care, the instinct for goodness, is a shining thread woven into the fabric of our being. As human beings we may tarnish the sheen or rend the fabric of our own goodness. We can act in cruel and heartless ways. But because we are human, we cannot completely rip out and destroy every vestige of the godliness by which and for which we were made. We cannot alter our essence. We are made by God, who is goodness itself. We are made like God. We are made for goodness.

The scripture that we read, the places we have been, the people we have seen, the evidence of science and our own life experience have convinced us that goodness is our essential quality. In the next chapter we will see that "being good" is the wrong goal. Attached to that notion of "being good" are all the "oughts" and "shoulds" that we think will win us the prize we truly crave: God's love and divine favor. We are wearing ourselves out in a quest to buy what is already ours: God's unmerited love. I will begin by sharing a very personal story about unmerited love.

But first turn with us into the stillness and listen to God speak with the voice of the heart:

My child, I made you for myself.
I made you like myself.
I delight in you.
My heart aches with pity
When you smother joy under the onslaught of busyness.
Then there is barely a minute
To pause and listen for me.

You run everywhere looking for life,
Searching for the life of life.
All the while I am here.
I am as close as a prayer.
I am breathing in your breath.

You look for me in the pleasures of life.
Things pile upon things,
Experiences crowd out experiences,
Places run together in a hazy blur,
And still you don't find that one thing that will satisfy you.
But I am here.
I am as close as a prayer.
I am breathing in your breath.

I made you for myself,
I wanted you.

I made you like myself,
I made you good and I made you free.

Listen! For I have carved in you the heart to hear.
Listen and know that I am near.
I am as close as a prayer.
I am breathing in your breath.

Before you speak the word of worry or worship I hear you.
Before you sing your delight or moan your anguish I speak.
I am here.
I am as close as a prayer.
I am breathing in your breath.

With each breath I choose life for you.
I paint the pattern of joy in your heart and leave it there for you to
*   find.*
I build the frame of your flourishing in the center of your being and
*   call you to search it out.*
I kindled the spark of goodness in you.
With each breath I fan the flame.
I am here.
I am as close as a prayer.
I am breathing in your breath.

With each breath you choose, my child, for you are free.
Will you breathe with me the breath of life?
Will you claim the joy I have prepared for you?
Will you seek me out and find me here?
Will you whisper the prayer?
Will you breathe in my breath?

2

STOP "BEING GOOD"

I dropped the phone and ran the two miles along the dusty streets to my parents' house. Racing through the warm midmorning, I could not contain my joy. "A son! We have a son!" In South Africa in 1956, birth was exclusively a woman's domain. There was no place for me to wait or to pace at the hospital, and so, controlling my anxiety, I stayed away. The Krugersdorp hospital was quite a distance from my parents' house. It was an inconvenient taxi ride from Munsieville, the black township where we lived. With my work schedule and no car, daily visits were out of the question. Telephones in the black township were few and far between. This one, at Nurse Belle's house, was the only one for miles around. On the morning after Leah was admitted to the hospital I made my first worried pilgrimage to the telephone to learn her progress. And now the hours of anxious waiting were washed away in a flood of elation and a surge of boundless love. Our blessing, our Thamsanqa, was born. Without as much as a glimpse of his face or a whiff of his milky breath I was in love. In the birth of this child I experienced something of the life of God. I experienced what it was to love without measure or merit. There was nothing for this child to do to earn my love. With his first breath he had captured my heart. I loved him because he was. I loved him for being.

Whether we are born from the loving union of two people or we are born under other circumstances doesn't matter. Whether our birth parents greeted our arrival with joyful anticipation or with fearful anxiety and regret is of no account. From the time before eternity our God has awaited each birth with love and delight. "Before I formed you in the womb I knew you" is the word of God to the Hebrew prophet Jeremiah. It is equally God's word to each of us. Before the "Let there be . . ." of creation, before God breathed Adam's first breath, God knew us and God loved us. God loves each of us as though there were no one else in the world, as though there were only one person to love.

We are so precious to God that, as Jesus reminds us in the pages of Matthew's Gospel, "even the hairs of your head are all counted." This is not only a word spoken to the disciples or to the Christian community down through the ages; it is God's word to all of humanity. Each of us is precious to God. This love that calls us into being and holds us in life is totally unmerited. God does not love us because we are lovable. We are lovable precisely because God loves us.

Before we could engage in any effort to earn God's love, it was given to us as gift. We get all worked up because we reckon that we must persuade God to love us. But God already loves and accepts us. God has loved us since the time before eternity. That love is God's gift to us.

In fact, everything is gift. There is nothing to earn. Unfortunately, somewhere along the line we have been inveigled and misled by the culture of achievement. We really can't understand unconditional acceptance. We think there must be a catch somewhere, so we tie ourselves in knots in the effort to impress God. We strive and strain to earn what is already ours. And it wears us out.

The annals of good works are bursting at the seams with tales of people who have burned themselves out. They haven't burned themselves out doing self-serving jobs. They have burned out doing work that needs to be done. Work we can all applaud. They have burned themselves out in the effort to promote justice and flourishing for all. These are people who have been dedicated and driven.

Not everyone who engages in this kind of work burns out. There are people with drive, energy, and passion who espouse just causes and find the work soul-sustaining and life-giving. And then there are people with equal drive, energy, and passion for whom the work becomes destructive. It's not the projects they take on that are destructive. It's not the dedication or passion that is destructive. Though their work may be motivated by passion for the particular cause and a deep-rooted concern for justice, for people who burn out, the work is also driven by a demon. The demon hidden behind the sense of purpose is a fear of not being good enough. It is the fear of not doing enough. That demon dread of not measuring up drains the joy from the work and saps the energy from the worker.

It is not only the so-called good works that can be driven by the invisible demon. The demon can kidnap any job and rob it of joy. When the demon steals into our psyche, the dedication and discipline that were once hallmarks of our devotion become an onerous burden. The tasks that once called us to give the best of ourselves, for the sheer pleasure of being involved in the work, come to feel like excessive demands. When the demon overtakes us we find that the career path that thrilled us when we first set our feet on it starts to meander through thickets of meaningless responsibilities, inane requirements, and mindless chores. When done in joyful love, the most mundane tasks can be life-affirming. When driven by the demon, the most exhilarating work can be numbingly life-denying.

What does it mean to live without the demon at your back? My spiritual brother His Holiness the Dalai Lama lives as one who knows. Since fleeing from the Chinese invasion of Tibet, the Dalai Lama has spent fifty years in exile in India. He has every reason to be a bitter old man. But he is both remarkably serene and boyishly mischievous. "Hey," I have to tell him, "the cameras are on us. Try to behave like a holy man." He is incorrigible!

There is no doubt at all when you meet him that you are

in a presence. He is patently holy. He is very disciplined. He does not work beyond a certain time at night, because he wakes early to meditate and pray. ("When I talk to myself" quips the patron deity of Tibet.) He is the exiled head of state of a country under foreign occupation. The resettlement policies of the Chinese government seem aimed at eradicating the national identity and culture of his people. These are weighty concerns, and the Dalai Lama approaches them with all due gravity and thoughtfulness. But he has not allowed the woes to overwhelm him. He can be so childlike in his playfulness. He carries in his being the essence of joy that is the gift of a person with nothing to prove.

How does the demon rob us of our joy? The demon fear of not being good enough convinces us that perfection is the price to pay for love. Our perfection is the price we imagine we must pay for the love of God. So we strive endlessly to "be good" or to "do good" instead of realizing that we *are* *good.* We don't have to struggle and strive to overcome an innate tendency to do what is bad and wrong. In everything we do we can fulfill the purpose for which we were made and rejoice in our inherent goodness. In short, we can stop "being good" and simply live from our goodness.

Goodness is not the coin with which we anxiously pay for God's love. Our goodness is, rather, the recognition we offer and the thanks we return for the gifts and the love already given us. Rather than a request for something yet to come, it is a response to the abundance of gifts that have already been given and received. It is in our makeup that, having been given, we want to give back. Having been loved, we want to be the best for our lover. I know that the space is very small between "I am doing it in response to love" and "I am doing it to be loved." But in that space resides the difference between joy-filled peace and anxious despair. In short, we don't have to "act" like a holy man or holy woman. We need to simply live out of the joy and generosity of our goodness.

When we slide across the threshold from living our goodness to "doing good" in order to "be good," we work in the mistaken conviction that what we are doing will enable us to merit God's love or that it will, perhaps, increase God's love for us. But God already loves us perfectly. There is no task we must complete to earn God's love. God already loves us perfectly; God cannot love us one iota more.

Equally, there is nothing we can do that will make God love us one iota less. The fourteenth-century English mystic Julian of Norwich wrote: "And I saw full certainly in this and in all the showings, that before God made us, He loved us and this love has never slackened nor ever shall be." When we falter, fail, or fall, when we don't measure up, we expect that God will smack us. We forget that, in many ways, it doesn't matter. God will still love us perfectly. It doesn't matter if we fall short, because it has no effect on God's love for us. It matters when we fall short because, as those who have received boundless love, we desire to return love and be a delight to our lover. When we falter, it is usually because we have been trapped into thinking that everything depends on us. When failure defeats us and drives us to despair, it is because our efforts were aimed at proving ourselves worthy—when, in fact, we have nothing to prove.

What is God's perfect love? How can we emulate it? Because none of us have mastered perfect love, it is almost impossible to conceive of such a love in God. Perfect love is not an emotion; it is not how we feel. It is what we do. Perfect love is action that is not wrapped up in self-regard, and it has no concern with deserving. Instead, perfect love is love poured out. It is self-offering made out of the joy of giving. It requires no prompting. It seeks no response and no reward. God's love is perfect because God always and only performs acts of love.

Recently the news media have been full of stories of marital infidelity. One man caught in the glare of the spotlight promised to rededicate himself to his marriage: "I am going to try to fall back in love with my wife." It was a disheartening vow. The older marriage liturgies, in their wisdom, do not require that you be "in love" with your spouse; after all, emotion is notoriously capricious and not within our power to control. But those liturgies do require that you love your partner. That is an altogether different thing. We cannot choose how we feel. We can choose what we do, how we act.

But we do not always act out of love. Sometimes we act out our anger. Sometimes we act out our shame. Sometimes we act out our jealousy, our insecurity, our pride, and our resentment. Sometimes we act out our hate. No, we do not love perfectly. But God does. And the more we come to emulate this divine love, the more our lives are an expression of the goodness that is at the heart of each of us.

The fifteenth chapter of Luke's Gospel in the Christian testament of the Bible has a series of parables—teaching stories that illustrate God's perfect love for us. Perfect love is seen in the example of the good shepherd who leaves ninety-nine sheep grazing contentedly on a hill to go in search of the one that has wandered away and is lost. Finding the lost sheep, the rejoicing shepherd carries it home on his shoulders as though the animal were a conquering hero rather than an obstreperous beast.

The father in the parable of the prodigal son shows perfect love. The boy demands his inheritance, and, selling this land, he moves to a far country, where he squanders his wealth on loose living. His fair-weather friends depart as the monies are depleted, and he is left destitute. He is brought very low. He is foraging for food in the pig slop when he comes to his senses. He decides to return to his father's home and express his remorse. He does not expect to be embraced as a son but hopes to be hired as a servant. While he is yet far off, his father sees him. The old man runs to greet his returning son. Barely are the words of apology out of the younger man's mouth than the father has embraced him and summoned servants to restore to his son the signs of his status: sandals, a robe, and a ring. The father calls for the fatted calf to be slaughtered in celebration of his son's return. The pain of his son's initial rejection and the years of absence have not diminished the father's love.

The prodigal son did not take his father's love for granted. He returned home expecting a kind of rejection from the father he had wronged. But as children, we often take our parents' love and their sacrifices for granted. A parent's sacrificial lack of self-regard is love made perfect.

I know that my mother made countless sacrifices on my behalf. There is one example that I remember vividly.

I was a student at the Johannesburg Bantu High School. It was one of only three high schools for black students on the West Rand at that time. Though it was the school closest to my home in Munsieville, the black township that served the white town of Krugersdorp, Bantu High School was still a forty-minute train ride away. In order to avoid the daily commute and save money, I was staying in the Community of the Resurrection hostel for young men in Sophiatown. From the hostel to the school was a fifteen-minute walk. Every two weeks or so, I would go home to Munsieville for the weekend.

There was one weekend when I went home for a visit. My father, Mkhulu, was home. I think he had taken leave but they hadn't paid him. Our family always lived paycheck to paycheck, and so, on this occasion, we were dependent on my mother's income. The weekend drew to a close, and it was time for me to return to school. I needed money for my train ticket. It probably cost only about two shillings to get a ticket from Krugersdorp to Westbury, the closest station to the hostel. We didn't have even that much money. So, on Monday morning I went with my mother to her white employer in town. My mother used to clean and do the washing and ironing for the white family for the princely sum of two shillings a day—enough money to buy half a pound of sugar, some cornmeal, and a serving of the cheapest meat for the evening meal.

On this Monday I went with her, and she was paid her wages before she worked. It didn't matter how she felt facing that long day of work. Love was what she did. She gave me the money for the train. After I left, she worked through the whole day, and at the end she had nothing. She had no money for the bus that usually carried her home at the end of the day. She would have to walk all the way. She would have no money to buy food for the evening meal or to pay her fare to work the following day.

My mother was not unique in this. There are mothers and fathers all around the world who work countless hours for practically nothing, just to put food on the family table. These are the daily examples of perfect love.

What are the qualities of perfect love?

Perfect love is the love that is responsive rather than re-active. It pays little or no regard to the emotions aroused in any given moment. We love perfectly when the good we do cares nothing for how we feel. When we love perfectly we endure beyond endurance. We pour ourselves out despite pain, stress, sadness, or fatigue. Perfect love is shown by the parent loving the unlovely child: waiting through the temper tantrum; holding and soothing the child through her vomiting; making the groggy midnight march to chase away the child's nightmares.

A nun of the Missionaries of Charity shows perfect love. She holds the stinking indigent so that even the most diseased poor may have a dignified dying. The founder of that order of nuns, Mother Teresa of Calcutta, said, "A beautiful death is for people who lived like animals to die like angels, loved and wanted."

Perfect love is shown by the people who deliver hot soup to prostitutes on cold nights, or blankets to street children. We can offer this love because we each have experienced it from God, though often unaware. We have experienced it in the rain that falls on our garden with no regard to whether we are deserving or not. We have experienced it in the gift of warm sunshine when our behavior merits a tempest. We have experienced it in the beauty of nature, the kindness of strangers, and the laughter of children. We have experienced it in the hundreds of graces that fill our days, though we have not earned them and do not deserve them.

That is why we Christians say we are called to be Eucharistic people, by which we mean we are called to be people filled with thanks: because we are always being given. Our goodness is our Eucharist. It is our thanksgiving for all that has been given to us.

Incredibly, the crisis of HIV/AIDS has created a South African Eucharist. It is a response to the crisis that is rooted in love and sustained by joyful thanksgiving. Mpho described an encounter in a black township outside Cape Town.

Gugulethu is not a pretty place. The houses are crowded together as though trying to shelter from the Cape wind: houses packed so close together that a conversation can be carried on from house to house almost as easily as from room to room. Few of the homes have running water. Even the ones with running water may boast only a standpipe in the yard. Many of the yards barely occupy three feet. In the part of Gugulethu that Mpho visited the gardens are not grass and flowers but earth packed down by the passage of many feet.

On a recent pilgrimage, Mpho took her group of pilgrims to visit Mrs. Maphosela. Her house stood on the thoroughfare to everywhere in a jumble of houses near the main road, the taxi rank, and the market. The middle-aged Mrs. Maphosela had started taking children into her home as their parents sickened, then died, from HIV/AIDS. First one dying mother asked her to take care of her child, then another. Then the children would be left at her door as ailing mothers saw that the children with Mama Maphosela were well cared for. When Mpho's group visited, the small three-room house was home to twenty children ranging in age from eight months to eighteen years. Most of the children were elementary school aged. Some of the children were infected with HIV, transmitted from mother to child in the birth canal. Most of the children were uninfected.

Even during the day, with many of the children playing outside, the house was cramped. The ten guests seemed to overwhelm the space. "I sleep in the bedroom with the girls. We move the chairs and tables from the kitchen for the boys to sleep," Mrs. Maphosela told Mpho. The corrugated metal shack that leans lazily against her house is a makeshift preschool and chapel. "I used to ride the taxi to church, but with all my children I can't afford it. Now a deacon comes to lead our worship here."

Some women from the neighborhood volunteer to help with cooking and other details of household management.

The children pitch in to help, the older ones taking care of the younger. A six-year-old balanced a toddler on her hip with practiced ease. The children looked clean, bright, well fed, and content.

For a long time, Mama Maphosela said she was not certain where the money would come from to cover the next bill, but somehow it was always there. Now her household is part of a study on the incidence of TB and HIV, and her income is more secure. When Mrs. Maphosela sat down, the children gathered close to her, clambering onto her lap, clinging to her knees, or snuggling under her arm. Somehow she managed to pat one child, hug another, wipe the runny nose of yet another, cuddle a baby, and kiss a toddler without interrupting the flow of her conversation. Each child seemed within easy reach of her affection. Though the work of caring for all these children could be overwhelming, Mama Maphosela has found love and thanks enough to fill the spaces in which anxiety could reside.

Perhaps the real miracle of Mrs. Maphosela is that she is not unique. In towns and townships all over South Africa, ordinary women are making the choice to live this Eucharist. None of them is wealthy. Few of them are well educated. All of them choose to live into their goodness. They open their hearts and homes to children with nowhere else to go.

Sometimes the demonstration of love in action can take us to dangerous places. Our love and our own goodness compel us to make choices that self-preservation would eschew. At a refugee camp in Darfur, I saw such heroism in the humanitarian relief workers. Almost all of them came from countries where they could have lived comfortably, safely, and securely. Yet here they were, quite a few of them, returning to the task for a second time. They came to a place where they were not secure, especially the women. They came to a place where they could be abducted, raped, killed. Nothing but love compelled their presence. Almost no one sang their praises. They came anyway.

The conditions under which people live in the camp are abominable. The shelters barely meet the definition of that word. They are not tents, or even shacks; they are flimsy structures made from sand. They do not protect from the heat of the North African sun. They do not protect against the bitter cold of the desert night. They afford the residents no privacy. The people there live almost like animals. If the women leave the confines of the camp, they run the serious risk of being abducted, raped, or killed. They are always open to attack. UNAMID—the joint United Nations–African Union peacekeeping force in Darfur—is inadequately armed. There is no safety in that place.

Darfur has come to symbolize so many of the ways we can be cruel, the ways we can be bad, and the things we do wrong. But even in this place the sheen of our innate goodness is impossible to obliterate. Despite all that squalor of the refugee camps, I saw Muslim men in gleaming white robes, their dignity unmarred by that supremely undignified place. I was surprised by the bubbles of laughter of the Darfuri women who gathered to talk with our group. These women—doctors, lawyers, and teachers in their lives before the terror, the war, and the camp—had profound wisdom to offer their compatriots in crafting a way out of the political morass that has overtaken the Sudan. Even the stresses and strictures of the refugee camp had not erased their capacity to delight in life. The fear and insecurity had not obliterated their ability to be touched by grace. The dignity of those men and the delight of those women were proof that our goodness is enduring.

Hearing stories like these can inspire us, but they can also induce in us feelings of guilt as we recognize that we are not doing as much as others, or perhaps even as much as we can. I share these stories because they tell us what we are capable of when we live out of our goodness. I certainly do not want to get your demon beating you up for not having done more. The point is to recognize that there is a Mrs. Maphosela in each of our hearts. There is a relief worker who resides in our soul. In each of us there is a dignified Darfuri, one who can find occasion for gratitude and joyful laughter in almost any circumstance. To whatever extent we recognize and act on those traits, they are there and want to be expressed. We can always aspire to be more compassionate and more generous, not out of some dogged need to be good or to be lovable, but because to give love is our greatest joy.

Does this mean that every act of Mrs. Maphosela's life is joyous? Absolutely not. Do the relief workers stay at great personal cost? You bet. Do the refugees in Darfur ever weep or worry? Of course. But if you ask any of them, they will tell you that there are immeasurable rewards that come from the goodness they live and the love they are able to give. They will tell you that selflessness opens a door to real peace.

How can we express this loving goodness in our own very ordinary lives? Loving with a lack of self-regard does not have to be heroic, nor does it have to happen half a world away, to be a valid expression of the goodness and compassion that are our essence. Child-care workers in the United States are ranked among those who earn the lowest wages in the country. Each day millions of young children spend most of their waking hours in the care of these people.

A teacher's lack of self-regard is one demonstration of love in action. Teachers set aside their own fatigue to care for the children in their charge. The parents who hand their children into the caregivers' charge trust the innate goodness of these workers. They expect that, no matter what these workers feel on any given day, their actions will speak of love.

In an orphanage, no parent will come to hold the caregivers to account. When the children are orphaned by strife or war, it is up to the adults to keep the divisions outside the walls of the facility. It is up to the adults to remember and to teach the disciplined art of love.

Natalie sits in an orphanage in Rwanda cuddling a small child to her breast. Natalie is a Tutsi woman. Her family was massacred by a Hutu mob in the genocide. The child she is holding is not her own. It is a Hutu child. Who knows if the child's parents are dead or if they have been imprisoned for their part in the slaughter? Perhaps this is the child of one of those responsible for the death of Natalie's family. No matter; Natalie says she is grateful to be alive. This person in her lap is alive and in need of comfort. This small act of love is Natalie's act of hope. A hug is such an ordinary gesture. It is repeated around the world a million times a day. Natalie's hug offers a testimony. The ordinary gift of a cuddle stands as witness to goodness. The child's goodness has not been erased by her people's deeds. Natalie's goodness allows her to see, in the face of one who might be considered an enemy, a child who is a good gift from the good God.

Half a world away another very ordinary act of parenting is its own prayer of thanksgiving. A tired Mpho sits beside her sick child. The long day of work blurs into a seemingly interminable night of rocking a feverish, fretful toddler back to sleep. The night rolls into another long, full day. As I listen to Mpho's report of her sleepless night, spent awake, comforting my sick grandchild, I see the person I was more than forty years ago rocking a feverish baby Mpho back to sleep. And we live our God-given goodness into the next generation.

Living our goodness is our way of testifying that we know ourselves to be perfectly loved by God. But as we will see in the next chapter, most of us grasp this truth only intellectually. Some of us are plagued by guilt and shame. Some of us tie ourselves in tortured knots in the dogged quest for a flawlessly perfect life. God invites us to set aside the guilt, the shame, and the anxious questing. We are invited to a different way of life—one that I first saw modeled in my grandmother's house. Come there with me.

But first turn with us into the stillness and listen to God speak with the voice of the heart:

Don't struggle and strive so, my child.
There is no race to complete, no point to prove, no obstacle course to
*   conquer for you to win my love.*
I have already given it to you.
I loved you before creation drew its first breath.
I dreamed you as I molded Adam from the mud.
I saw you wet from the womb.
And I loved you then.

Take my yoke upon you and learn from me, for my yoke is easy and
*   my burden is light.*
Stop racing ahead at your own pace;
*   you will only be exhausted, flamed out, and spent before the task*
*   is accomplished.*
Pace yourself with me; walk alongside me.

Do you think I don't know the demands of your life?
I see you striving for perfection, craving my acceptance.
I see you bending yourself out of shape to conform to the image that
*   you have of me.*
Do you imagine that I did not know who you were when I made
*   you, when I knit you together in your mother's womb?*
Do you think I planted a fig tree and expected roses to bloom?
No, child, I sowed what I wanted to reap.

You are a child after my own heart.
Seek out your deepest joy and you will find me there.
Find that which makes you most perfectly yourself and know that I
*   am at the heart of it.*
Do what delights you

And you will be working with me,
Walking with me,
Finding your life
Hidden in me.

Ask me any question.
My answer is love.
When you want to hear my voice,
Listen for love.
How can you delight me?
I will tell you:
Love.
The tough, unbreakable, unshakable love.
Are you looking for me?
You will find me in love.
Would you know my secrets?
There is only one:
Love.
Do you want to know me?
Do you yearn to follow me?
Do you want to reach me?
Seek and serve love.

3

AN INVITATION TO WHOLENESS

I really looked forward to going to Stirtonville to be with my maternal grandmother. Stirtonville was the township that served as the black dormitory for the white town of Boksburg. In apartheid South Africa all white towns had a black township that served that function. We lived in Munsieville, outside the white town of Krugersdorp. The hour-long train ride from Krugersdorp to Boksburg was exciting for me as little boy. It signaled the beginning of the Christmas holiday, that long summer break from school. The whole family would go to Stirtonville. My father was the principal of the elementary school in Munsieville. In the summer he took work as a delivery boy at a bottle store (liquor store) in Boksburg to earn some extra money.

My grandmother, Kuku, did laundry for a white family in town. One of the things I remember so vividly was that my cousins and I would sit waiting for her at the end of the day. She came back in the late afternoon, around four or five o'clock. When we saw her rounding the corner we'd run to meet her. She would pretend to slap us away from her: "Get off me, you little dogs!" Yet this person who cursed us so roundly had brought us the incomparable treat of bread and jam, the breakfast her employer had given her. She hadn't eaten her morning meal. She had saved it for us.

Strangely, it never occurred to me that we were poor. We didn't have many toys—hardly any, in fact. I remember a ball and the cars we would construct from scraps of wire and empty boot-polish tins. There was an ice-cream truck that came around. It was a special treat to be given a penny with which to purchase an ice-lolly. One of the great joys we had was that every now and then there was a free movie at night—such box-office greats as *Tea Is Good for You!* I think the excitement was that it came around only once in a while.

I don't remember noticing that the house in Stirtonville was overcrowded. It can't have had more than four rooms. Over Christmas it had to accommodate eight of us: my father and mother, my grandmother, two cousins, my two sisters, and me. The house was made of corrugated metal. It wasn't a shack: it had proper walls inside. But the outside was metal, and the floors were compacted dirt, something akin to adobe. We shared a communal bucket-toilet with three or four families on our street. Twice each day we would line up at the communal tap to fill our buckets with water for cooking, cleaning, personal hygiene, and any other household needs. The house stood on an ample plot of land. On one side was a vegetable garden; my grandmother grew corn and pumpkins and, sometimes, carrots or spinach. Our family was very house-proud; it seemed everyone was, back then. The house and yard were swept daily. We even used to sprinkle water to damp down the dust and then sweep the street in front of our house.

Looking back now from the comfort of our Cape Town home with its bright, beautiful rooms and gleaming bathrooms, I can see our lack, but to me, growing up, the house in Stirtonville was perfect. It was a place in which we could live a good life. It was a home that was loved in. Our life in Stirtonville did not meet the usual definition of perfection. But our life in that place was whole. Caring and concern filled the gaps that circumstance created.

In the previous chapter, we established that we do not have to force ourselves toward goodness. In this chapter we want to make it clear that we do not need to conform ourselves to an anxious flawlessness. Indeed, the perfection that is available to us is quite different than the impossible measure by which we so often judge ourselves.

The perfection of that Stirtonville home is the kind of perfection that is in God's invitation to us and in Jesus's command to the Christian. "Be perfect, therefore, as your Father in heaven is perfect" we read in the text of Matthew's Gospel. Read through the lens of our daily human experience, the command seems like a recipe for stress and anxiety. So many of us struggle just to be good enough. The command to be perfect seems to put living into our true godliness outside the realm of possibility.

What do you hear when I say the word *perfect?* Do you, like most of us, hear something beyond your reach? In the word *perfect* you might hear every test you failed. You might hear every target you did not quite hit. You might hear the impossible standard set for you by a parent, teacher, partner, or spouse. Indeed you might hear the impossible standard you set for yourself. As you read "Be perfect," you may find your stomach coiling into an anxious knot as you wonder what is now to be demanded of you that you cannot achieve. As human beings, we hear in the command to be perfect a demand for flawlessness. *But flawlessness is not the goal of God's invitation.*

Mpho is familiar with the clenched stomach and gritted teeth of the human striving for perfection. She travels extensively as a public speaker, preacher, and teacher. As the mother of young children, she often has one or both of her girls in tow. She tells me that she knows she's lost the prize for parenting perfection as she boards a plane with a screaming toddler and half the people she addressed at her most recent conference.

I suspect that the image of parenting perfection is one held in her mind—not necessarily a vision held by the other parents or anyone else on the plane. She is not the first mother to try to soothe a tot in midmeltdown. And many a father would meet her eye with the sympathetic smile of common experience. No earthly parent has yet achieved the perfection after which generations of human parents have quested.

Each generation finds a new focus for its anxious yearning. In our world our self-worth seems so bound up in outdoing each other. We have this arbitrary set of standards against which we are constantly measuring ourselves, and we never measure up. There is the standard of what we are supposed to earn—and that is invariably more than we are actually making. There is the measure of the size of our home or our bank account or any one of a number of seemingly important assets or attributes. Of course we always know someone with a bigger house, a bigger bank account, a better car, better wardrobe, or better figure. It seems that their children are on the honor roll, playing the impossible musical instrument, leading the dance troupe, and starring in the school play. Somehow we are always falling down on the job. Heard through the filter of our competing and striving, the command to be perfect feels like one more impossible demand on a long list of impossible demands. Rather than an invitation to greater joy, it sounds like another place to fail.

But God's call to be perfect is not just a command—it is an invitation. It is an invitation to something possible. It is an invitation to something life-giving, to something joy-creating. God invites us to a godly perfection. Godly perfection is not flawlessness. Godly perfection is wholeness.

We can learn some of the contours of wholeness from people who fully inhabit their own lives regardless of the circumstances of their lives.

Mpho says she learned something of the shape and substance of wholeness from the women of the St. Philip's Mothers' Union. She joined the group when she was a seminarian in Grahamstown, South Africa. The women came from many walks of life and from all over the economic spectrum. Some were professionals or retired professionals, mainly teachers and nurses. Some owned small businesses. Some were domestic workers. Some were unemployed. Many, as was the pattern in the black township of Rhini, were underemployed.

Each Thursday these women would gather to pray, sing, study the Bible, and reflect on their lives. The reflections were self-revelatory. There was no pretense at flawlessness. All the hardships and disappointments of life were shared there. Worries about a child's health, concerns about a husband's infidelity, cares about work were all heard in that gathering. All the joys of life were brought to that congregation too. Thanksgiving for an unexpected windfall, happiness about the birth of a grandchild, relief at the resolution of a family dispute—all these things were part of the mosaic of life that the community of women described.

They responded to each other candidly. They offered support and comfort to each other in hard times. They provided prayerful guidance in perplexity. They challenged each other to move out of complacency. When the path of goodness was obscured by the tangles of pain, shame, or failure, they cleared the way with their collective wisdom. They rejoiced together when any one of them enjoyed a special blessing. Even the flaws, failures, and limitations of their lives were part of the pattern of godliness. By their example, they taught each other how to live lives of wholeness, lives of goodness. They learned together how to live lives of godly perfection.

God is not calling on us to create the museum-quality house, the magazine-ready garden, and the immaculate self-presentation. A life that can be completely described by "I," "me," and "my" may look flawless, but it is not a life of godly perfection. God's invitation to perfection is a call to a truly good life. The good life means flourishing for us and for others.

By the measures of worldly privilege, prestige, and human success, my friend the late Beyers Naudé had the "perfect" life. Beyers was an Afrikaner cleric. He was born into the royalty of Afrikanerdom. His father was a founding member of the secretive and politically powerful Afrikaner Broederbond. The Broederbond was group that was committed to preserving apartheid to secure the interests of Afrikaners. Beyers became the youngest member of the Broederbond at the age of twenty-five. He was the dominee, or leader, of a prestigious Johannesburg Dutch Reformed congregation. He was also the moderator of the Southern Transvaal synod of the Dutch Reformed Church (DRC).

But his seemingly perfect life was built on an untenable foundation. The South African DRC had constructed the theological pillars on which apartheid was established. Beyers's prayer, study, and reflection had led him to conclude that apartheid was unbiblical and unchristian and that its effects were indefensible. Forced to choose between the multiracial Christian Institute that he had created and the Dutch Reformed Church that he had led and loved, Beyers chose obedience to conscience. One Sunday in September 1963 he announced his decision to his congregation. "We must show greater loyalty to God than to man," he said. He hung his gown on the pulpit and walked out of the church. He resigned his post as moderator of his church district, left his congregation, and, as a result, lost his status as a minister in the DRC. His fellow Afrikaners ostracized him and his family.

It seemed that his life was in ruins. But Beyers had traded in what looked like a flawlessly perfect life for a perfectly whole life—a life that he could fully inhabit. Although his Afrikaner community abandoned him, South Africa's black community embraced him. He joined a black Dutch Reformed congregation in Alexandra Township. Friends of all races filled his home. Pastors from every denomination sought his counsel. Antiapartheid activists met with him for mutual support.

Over the years Beyers faced government harassment. His Christian Institute was outlawed. For seven years he was placed under a banning order. Banning was a form of punishment that was akin to house arrest. The banning order made it illegal to quote Beyers in any publication. Banning also meant that he could not be in a room with more than one other person, so he could not take part in family gatherings or attend a service of worship. His period in the wilderness lasted more than thirty years. Beyers's views were vindicated when Nelson Mandela became South Africa's first democratically elected president. Beyers spent the last five years of his life as a worshiper at Aasvoëlkop, the Johannesburg congregation that had first heard his declaration of conscience. He had dared to stand as a solitary witness against the injustice perpetrated by his people. He had traded a false perfection for godly wholeness.

As I described earlier, in our own South African lexicon godly perfection is described by the multifaceted concept of "*ubuntu.*" *Ubuntu* recognizes the interconnectedness of life. My humanity, we say, is bound up with your humanity. One consequence of *ubuntu* is that we recognize that we all need to live our lives in ways that ensure that others may live well. Our flourishing should enhance the lives of others, not detract from them. In the 1980s, American college students showed *ubuntu* when, on college campuses across the United States, they halted their studies to protest U.S. investment in apartheid South Africa. Their demonstrations provided the students no discernible benefit. But they provided a very real comfort to black South Africans, a very real challenge to a popular U.S. president, Ronald Reagan, and a warning to the apartheid government that its days were numbered.

God's invitation to wholeness always includes more than ourselves. God's invitation to wholeness is *ubuntu.*

For example, we are becoming more aware of the impact of our use of natural resources on the global environment. We are learning that fuel use in the United States affects sea levels in Fiji. Carbon emissions in India affect asthma in Iceland. The propellants and refrigerants used in many parts of the world are punching a hole in the ozone layer that will affect all of us. Our misuse of the earthly environment has been in the pursuit of a human vision of worldly perfection. We use what we want as we will, because it seems to create the greatest benefit for our smallest circle of concern: "I," "me," and "my."

This human vision of perfection—this quest for more, bigger, faster—is not the perfection in God's dictionary. Muslim carpet weavers come closer to the ideal of godly perfection. They deliberately incorporate a flaw into each work of art that they create. Only God, they say, is flawless. Only God can create flawlessness. So they do not strive for flawlessness; they strive, instead, for beauty.

The invitation to godly perfection, God's invitation to wholeness, is an invitation to beauty. It is God's invitation to us to be life artists, to be those who create lives of beauty. Out of the cacophony of random suffering and chaos that can mark human life, the life artist sees or creates a symphony of meaning and order. A life of wholeness does not depend on what we experience. Wholeness depends on *how* we experience our lives.

In a life of wholeness, a life of godly perfection, we will still confront the death, grief, and pain that are part of human reality, but they will not destroy us. A life of wholeness can accept, even embrace, death, grief, and pain. They are essential parts of the fabric of life. They lend texture to life.

In a life of wholeness, we will endure failures. And we will come to know so many of our own flaws. But that will not defeat us. A life of wholeness can meet failure as the wisest teacher. A life of wholeness can accept flaws and vulnerabilities as doors to relationship. If we can do all things flawlessly, we have no need of anybody else. That is not *ubuntu*. Flaws and vulnerabilities destroy the illusion of self-sufficiency and can open our eyes to our common humanity. Flaws and vulnerabilities can build the bridge to human community and to a relationship with the divine.

In a life of wholeness we may face brokenness and endure woundedness, but our suffering will not be meaningless. Meaningless suffering is soul-destroying.

Time and again I have been with people who have undergone unspeakable anguish. I have listened to people who have been subjected to brutal torture. I have sat with people who have borne terrible loss. Some could find no meaning in their suffering. Years after the horror had passed, the memories still held them hostage. Others, like my former colleague Tom Manthata, possessed a freedom that was theirs even as the apparatus of the state held them bound in chains.

Tom was a senior staff member of the South African Council of Churches when I was the council's general secretary. He spent almost a year in "preventive detention." He was held without trial for more than two hundred days. He was tortured while in police custody. When he came out of prison he spoke to his friends in the Council of Churches. "Let us not be consumed by bitterness," he said. He spoke of how his experience inched us closer to a postapartheid future. Tom may not be described as an artist in the ordinary sense, but he wove meaning for all of us from the threads of his suffering.

There are times or experiences that can seem to define beauty. Tom's time in jail would not fit that definition. In crafting meaning from that time, Tom gathered up the horror that he had endured and made of it something truly beautiful.

There are houses that we readily describe as beautiful. They are photographed for the covers of home and garden magazines. The house in Stirtonville would not fit that definition of beauty, but it was beautiful for the love that was shared within its walls. The photographers for a men's fashion magazine might pass the lanky Trevor Huddleston without a second glance. No flawless mien would meet their eye. He met none of their criteria for beauty, but he was a man who presence brought the beauty of love to some very ugly places.

Huddleston was an Englishman. He was an Anglican priest, a monastic, and, when our paths first crossed, the Priest-in-Charge of the Sophiatown and Orlando missions of the Community of the Resurrection. He later became the provincial, or head, of that monastic order in Southern Africa.

I was standing with my mother outside the building where she was working at the time. I was nine or ten years old. She was a cook at Ezenzeleni, a facility for black blind women. We were enjoying the faint warmth of the winter sun when a white man in a long cassock swept past and doffed his hat to my mother. When it happened, I didn't realize that it had made such an impression on me. But a white man doffing his hat to my mother, a black woman, in 1940s apartheid South Africa was an unbelievable gesture. I subsequently met him and discovered that he had a profound belief in the doctrine of creation. He truly believed that we are each equally created in the image of God. He lived as he believed. Conscience met action in a gesture of godly perfection. For him it was the most natural thing to do: doff his hat to another child of God.

Trevor was an astonishing man. He was like the pied piper. When he walked on the streets of Sophiatown, his white cassock would not stay spotless for long; the children ran to grasp his hand or hold on to his cassock. "Fadder, Fadder" ("Father, Father"), they would call, wanting a word, a touch, or a smile. It seemed the world walked through his office at 74 Mercer Street. One moment he would have a number of small boys, almost street urchins, like us playing marbles on the floor of his office. The next moment he would be meeting with mining magnate Harry Oppenheimer of De Beers. I saw the same years later when I, by then bishop of Lesotho, visited his office in London when he was bishop of Stepney. He had to usher a gaggle of children out of his office so we could meet in private.

Trevor loved music and fostered in the children who gathered around him a similar love. He introduced us to classical music. He brought the violinist Yehudi Menuhin to perform at Christ the King in Sophiatown. When I met Lord Menuhin in San Francisco many years later, I told him that I was a small boy in the township when I first heard him play. Trevor touched the lives of so many people with his concern. People like Hugh Masekela, who is one of our leading jazz trumpeters. Hugh got his first trumpet from Louis Armstrong through Trevor Huddleston.

A few years after I first met Trevor Huddleston he brought his unique grace to a place that I hated. A hospital. It is one place that is particularly horrible to me. It is my pet hate. I spent a seemingly interminable twenty months in hospital. I must say that although I hate hospitals, I do love nurses. I fell in love with my nurse in 1947 when, at the age of fifteen, I first got tuberculosis. That was at Coronation Hospital, outside Soweto. After a month there, I was moved to the TB hospital in Rietfontein. And in those twenty months, almost every week Trevor Huddleston visited me in hospital. It is very difficult to explain what it meant to a black ghetto urchin to have an important white man do this. In the beauty he created and the beauty he helped us to create, Trevor lived a perfect life, a life of genuine wholeness. A life in which action and belief were all of a piece.

Tom, and Trevor, my family in Stirtonville—these examples of godly perfection have a common recognition: holiness is not a solo quest. Even the solitaries of ancient memory and modern description do not account themselves as people who are alone. The Desert Fathers and Mothers relied on their spiritual strength and a firm recognition of the presence of God to sustain their solitude. Those who withdraw to the wilderness become keenly aware of the companionship of the plants, birds, and animals that make their homes in the places that other human beings have not yet populated.

The Bible offers God's companionship for the journey. "Take my yoke upon you and learn from me," Jesus says in Matthew's Gospel. In the rush of modern life, these are words we need to hear. "My yoke is easy and my burden is light." God invites us not only to a different way of doing, but to a different way of being. We are invited to be at home in our own lives.

What does it mean to be at home in our own lives? Ideally, our physical homes are the places where we shed all striving and pretense. They are the places where no artifice is required in our self-presentation. Being at home in our own lives is a kindred experience. When we are at home in our lives, thought and action are all of a piece.

In our early years in England, while I was a student at King's College, London, I served as a part-time curate at St. Alban's in Golders Green. We lived in a cramped little curate's flat a stone's throw from the parish church. The verger lived downstairs. We knew that our four young children had been particularly rowdy when the verger and his family passed us in the vestibule without giving a greeting. We had very little money. Sometimes our money ran out well before the month was done.

We made lifelong friends in England. Some of them were among the landed aristocracy. Some were regular guests at Buckingham Palace. They had space aplenty in their homes and could afford to have the choicest food at their tables. When they gathered around our table, Leah would cook a pot of the South African staple, *mnqusho* (a seasoned mix of beans and hominy), about the cheapest food one could make, and offer a bottle of inexpensive wine (on the days that the budget stretched that far), and our friends would squeeze into the available space and relish the repast as though it were sweeter than manna. We could not pretend at human perfection. Our friends' sophisticated palates could immediately discern the quality of the wine. The decor in our flat was far from flawless. But it was not the food or the place but the welcome that made the feast.

In the years since then, Leah and I have entertained priests and princes, paupers, tycoons, and movie stars in the mansions my bishoprics have provided. Leah, at home in life as she is at home in the houses we have called home, welcomes each person with that unique brand of warmth and grace that can turn the most meager meal into a feast and can turn any feast into a banquet.

We have explored how we can become life-artists. We can create lives of beauty that have space for the flaws and failures that are an inevitable part of the human experience. Creating a life of beauty is a choice. We are given the freedom to choose how we will use the gifts and challenges that we are given. In the next chapter we will explore that freedom. I will begin by telling you about a fateful choice.

But first turn with us into the stillness and listen to God speak with the voice of the heart:

> Take my yoke upon you and learn from me, for my yoke is easy and my burden is light.
> Match your pace to mine, imitate me.
> You are free to choose, you can choose to be like me.
> Wherever you are you can create beauty.
> Moment by moment you can create joy.
> Instant by instant you can offer kindness.

Now and always you can make me seen.
You can be as I created you to be,
The visible likeness of the invisible.
You will see as I see.
And your heart will break
For all the sadness in the world.
For all the hunger and pain.
You will cry every tear with me
And share every joy with me.

You will see every sparrow fall.
You will see each dying blade of grass.
You will hear every child's cry and every father's despairing sigh.
The terrified screams and hungry moans will be woven into the song
    of who you are and your heart will be broken and broken again.
And then you know a heart of flesh and not a heart of stone.
You will be alive!

4

FREE TO CHOOSE

*L*izalis'idinga lako, Tixo, Nkosi yenyaniso." The song rang out with a mixture of pain and defiance. The man standing next to me was belting out all six verses of the Christian hymn from memory. "Fulfill Your Purpose, Lord God of Truth" seemed an unlikely anthem for this man to know so well or to sing so lustily. We were in Bisho—the capital of the nominally independent Ciskei homeland—at yet another of the funerals that marked the horribly hazardous road to the new South Africa. The man who stood beside me singing in full voice was Chris Hani. He had recently retired as the chief of staff of uMkhonto we Sizwe (Spear of the Nation), the armed wing of Mandela's African National Congress (ANC), and was now the general secretary of the South African Communist Party. I gave him a sidelong glance. "Aren't you a godless Communist?" I asked. "I think the newspapers called you the Antichrist. You are not living up to your billing!"

"Oh," he responded with his characteristic warm smile, "I was an altar boy. I wanted to be a Roman Catholic priest."

If you had polled South Africa's black population in 1992, Chris Hani would have been second only to Nelson Mandela in popularity. Chris's biography had captured the imagination of the militant township youth. He had been on the run from the hated South African security police. He had been captured but escaped and fled into exile. He had joined the MK—uMkhonto we Sizwe—and risen swiftly through the ranks. As a foot soldier he fought alongside Zimbabwe's ZIPRA liberation forces against Rhodesian and South African soldiers who were determined to maintain the stranglehold of apartheid. As a senior commander in the MK he had survived an assassination attempt. The bomb intended for Hani had detonated in his assailant's hand. All of these facts burnished his image among the "comrades."

The "comrades"—the young black men who populated South Africa's urban townships—were impatient for change, and they saw in Hani a man of action. They trusted his leadership. They held their fire at Hani's command. While they honored and revered Mandela, Chris inspired a different expression of fealty. He made them feel powerful even as he had them stay their hands.

Unlike Mandela, who was a Thembu prince, Chris was a commoner with the common touch. His mother was an illiterate sharecropper, his father a semiliterate worker in the building industry. As a young boy growing up in the

Transkei region of South Africa, Chris walked fifteen miles to school each week and almost as far to serve at the Roman Catholic Church on Sundays. Campaigning in rural communities around South Africa, Chris was able to build support for the South African Communist Party because his personal history was so similar to the lives of his audiences.

With his support for the suspension of military activity in favor of a negotiated end to apartheid, he had gained the guarded respect of many white South Africans. His charm, political acuity, and warm personality helped him to garner the admiration of the diverse group of negotiating partners who were now working toward an end to apartheid and the institution of a nonracial democracy in South Africa. Still, the path of negotiation was anything but smooth.

The euphoria that had greeted the release of Nelson Mandela and the unbanning of liberation organizations in 1990 had evaporated in a seemingly unending spiral of violence and a negotiating process that moved in fits and starts. The first round of talks, CODESA (Convention for a Democratic South Africa) I, had ended in December 1991. Between the end of the first round of talks and the beginning of the second round, the situation in the country had deteriorated sharply. Violence in the black townships had escalated, and the ANC suspected the South African security police of fomenting the unrest. The second round of meetings, CODESA II, began in May 1992.

The atmosphere surrounding the negotiations was tense. White South Africans had very little reason to be sanguine about their security under a postapartheid government.

Many of them were preparing to emigrate to Europe, the Americas, Australia, or New Zealand. The leaders of the white-government-constructed reservations or "homelands" were concerned about how they would fare in any new dispensation. The "homeland" leaders were generally regarded as collaborators with the apartheid regime. Their claimed independence was beneficial only to the apartheid government and the leaders themselves. That "independence" was detrimental to their "subjects," black South Africans who were stripped of their South African citizenship and made citizens of these "independent homelands." The citizens of an "independent homeland" could not claim the rights of a citizen in South Africa.

In the black townships around Johannesburg the tensions that had always existed between the migrant hostel dwellers, most of them from the "homelands," and the permanent residents were exacerbated by the refusal of the "homeland" leaders to participate in the talks. A series of violent attacks by hostel dwellers on taxi and train riders commuting to the cities to work had created an edgy township population.

In June 1992 Zulu migrant workers from the KwaMadala hostel attacked residents of the black township of Boipatong. Forty-six people were killed. The Boipatong massacre marked a new low point as Mandela accused F. W. de Klerk's government of complicity in the slaughter. The ANC withdrew from CODESA and called for "rolling mass action." The people responded by taking their protests to the streets. In September 1992 in Bisho in the Ciskei, one of the "independent homelands," the Ciskei army opened fire on a crowd of demonstrators. Twenty-eight people were killed. Chris and I stood together in Bisho to memorialize the fallen. In the wake of that bloodshed the parties recognized the urgent need for a political solution and resumed negotiations. By the end of September the ANC and the government had agreed on a Record of Understanding that formed the basis for the next round of talks.

In April 1993 there was a faint new hope for a negotiated end to apartheid. On April 1 the Multi-Party Negotiating Forum met. This group consisted of representatives from the government and the ANC. Representatives from the "home-land governments," conservative white parties, traditional leaders, and delegations from the Pan Africanist Congress and other groups that had either refused to participate in or had been excluded from previous talks also joined this forum. That frail hope for peace was almost shattered two weeks later.

It was Easter Eve, April 10, 1993. Dawn Park, a recently integrated suburb of Johannesburg, was lazily entering into Saturday morning. This place was a foretaste of the new South Africa. Rabid racists who were bent on preserving apartheid were neighbors to people who had endured jail, torture, and exile in their commitment to end that system of government. Afrikaans and Xhosa, English and seTswana—some of the wealth of languages with which South Africa is blessed—were on the lips of homeowners in Dawn Park. That would have been impossible three short years before, when segregation was the law of the land and only white people had the right to own property in South Africa or to live in that suburb. Dawn Park was the place that Chris Hani and his wife, Limpho, had made their home.

On this Saturday Limpho was not home. She was visiting family in the neighboring kingdom of Lesotho. As was his wont, Chris had dismissed his bodyguards. It wasn't that he was unconcerned for his own safety. Rather, as he had told his friend and neighbor, Jon Qwelane, "Look, Jon, this is *my* country as well. . . . If death comes, so be it, but I will not imprison myself in my own country." Chris drove to the nearby shopping center to buy bread and the morning paper. He didn't notice the car that was following him. When Chris returned home, Januz Waluz pulled into the driveway behind him. As he stepped out of the car carrying his groceries Waluz called out to him, "Mr. Hani?"

A shot rang out and Chris fell to the ground, blood pouring from his mouth and nose. The gunman approached and fired one more time. The fatal bullet struck Chris behind his left ear. Nomakhwezi, Chris's thirteen-year-old daughter, heard the shots and ran outside to find her father dying, his blood soaking into the African soil. Her frantic screams echoed around the neighborhood.

A neighbor, Retha Harmse, was pulling out of her driveway as the shots were fired and managed to jot down the license number of the departing car. She ran back into her house to telephone the police with the information. Ten minutes later an alert patrolman spotted the vehicle passing the city hall in Boksburg. He stopped the car and detained the driver.

Januz Waluz was a Polish immigrant and anti-Communist zealot. He recognized that South Africa was poised on a powder keg of political tension. He felt certain that Chris's death would ignite a conflagration that South Africa would not be able to extinguish. He could have been right. The road to nonracial, truly democratic elections had been marred by so many horrors. The rage and violence that had simmered under the surface of the apartheid state found expression in bloody battles in black townships, in massacres that were either executed or orchestrated by the apartheid security apparatus, and in murders, massacres, and assassinations in the rural communities of the homelands. South Africa was indeed a powder keg. Into this volatile atmosphere was cast the match of Chris Hani's death.

In an unprecedented act F. W. de Klerk's apartheid government, which still controlled the major news outlets, invited Nelson Mandela to address the nation. It was more than a year before the elections that would make Mandela president. In fact, the date for those historic elections had not yet been set. Nelson Mandela did not have the military power, nor did he control any of the other symbols of the presidency, but he had all the authority of that office. His speech and his mien were clearly presidential.

"Tonight I am reaching out to every single South African, black and white, from the very depths of my being. A white man, full of prejudice and hate, came to our country and committed a deed so foul that our whole nation now teeters on the brink of disaster. A white woman, of Afrikaner origin, risked her life so that we may know, and bring to justice, this assassin. The cold-blooded murder of Chris Hani has sent shock waves throughout the country and the world. . . . Now is the time for all South Africans to stand together against those who, from any quarter, wish to destroy what Chris Hani gave his life for—the freedom of all of us."

The country teetered on the brink of chaos. The week that followed Hani's death was marked by rallies and protests, memorial services, and mass gatherings of every kind. The poisonous brew of rage and grief simmered ominously. But Mandela's words and his daily appearances on the television news, on the front pages of the country's newspapers, and on the radio tamed the tone of the assemblies. The widespread bloody riots that seemed inevitable were absorbed into the story of South Africa. Instead of fuel for an all-consuming fire, Chris's death became a catalyst for change.

Although F. W. de Klerk was still the president of the country through that tense week of commemorative actions, as Mandela's image filled South Africa's television screens the country recognized that Nelson Mandela was the legitimate leader. Chris Hani's death became the source of a renewed urgency in the negotiations to end apartheid.

Nelson Mandela had a choice. In the midst of frustrating negotiations for an end to apartheid, and in the face of the mounting casualty count of his black constituents, Mandela could have called for war. Chris Hani was a colleague, an adviser, and a friend. His death was an outrage that demanded an answer. The answer could have been wrath and revenge. But Mandela had the courage to call for peace. In a moment of utmost volatility, Mandela chose to use his authority to damp the flames of bloody fury. He chose the long-term good of the country above the immediate satisfaction of demanding revenge.

Not all of our choices are quite so historical. They are, nonetheless, consequential. Choice is a freedom each person has. God invests each of us with the freedom to choose. It is a very real freedom. We have the freedom to choose right. But that would be meaningless if there were not also the possibility that we would choose wrong. If there were no potential for evil, then our God-given freedom would be like the offerings of the old Ford Motor Company: "You can choose any color as long as it's black." A choice that is no choice at all.

At least as far back as biblical times, human beings have grappled with the reality of choice. The writers of the Bible were concerned to tell us that choice was a part of God's gift to us in creation. We are not the props of a celestial puppet master. We are creatures with agency. We are creatures who can affect the course of creation. The writers of the book of Genesis illustrate the reality of our gift and explore the consequences in the story of Adam and Eve in the Garden of Eden. In that tale God created a garden in Eden as a dwelling place for the humans. God gave the humans freedom to live in the garden as they saw fit but made one restriction. As long as Adam and Eve chose to honor God's prohibitions, all would be well. They could live in the certainties of paradise. But for the freedom to be meaningful, it had to be possible for them to ignore God's instructions. The authors made the serpent in the idyllic garden the metaphor for doubt.

"Don't eat the fruit of the tree in the middle of the garden. Don't even touch it or you will die!"

Eve reports God's injunction to the serpent.

"You will not die; for God knows that when you eat of it your eyes will be opened, and you will be like God, knowing good and evil." The serpent tempts first woman, and first woman "saw that the tree was good for food, and that it was a delight to the eyes, and that the tree was to be desired to make one wise, she took of its fruit and ate; and she also gave some to her husband, who was with her, and he ate."

For their disobedience Adam, Eve, and the serpent are expelled from Eden.

With that awakening of knowledge and the ability to choose, the absolutes of paradise can no longer contain human beings. We must live with the banes and blessings of freedom, the gifts and the consequences of our choices. God could have created us to be automatons, programmed to do the right thing. Instead God took the incredible risk of saying that we are persons. We have a real autonomy. That autonomy may be limited in comparison to God's autonomy, but it is real.

The freedom to choose wrong is not only biblical; it is also very topical. It is part of every person's lived experience. Dieters succumb to the lure of chocolate cake, spendthrifts break the budget for that one-time bargain, the daredevil ignores the stop sign or runs the red light. Our children choose each day whether they will hew to their parent's teaching or wander away onto the paths that will impress, or even just let them fit in with, their peers.

"Why?" we ask as we look at yet another human-wrought landscape of disaster or devastation. "Why did God let this happen?" The territory that confronts us may be the mangled aftermath of a terrorist bombing or the trail of wreckage a drunk driver leaves in his wake. It might be the famished bodies of the children of war or the ravaged faces of the victims of torture that provoke our distressed "Why?" What kind of God would let these things happen? A God who will not violate our freedom.

God has a profound reverence for our freedom. Because of this regard, God will not send an angel with a flaming sword to stand before us to turn us away from our chosen path. I often say that God would rather we go freely to hell than that we be compelled to enter heaven. Even if God does send messengers to challenge us, it is still possible that we will overrun them in our determination to achieve our evil ends. Yet even at that moment, the moment when we have bent our wills to evil, God is as close as our breath, loving us and willing us to turn aside, but God wills our change of heart in such a way that God does not undermine our autonomy.

The depth of God's reverence for human autonomy is difficult to fathom in the abstract. It is hard to grasp when presented as a simple assertion. Jesus conveyed God's regard for our freedom in the parable of the prodigal son. When our children were growing up, that parable, especially the end of the story, gripped me. Through all the trials and turmoils of

parenting, I was sustained by the vision of the father's un-
failing love. I had the pattern of that father's forgiveness to
chide and challenge me. I had the vision of that father's reverence for his child's autonomy to stay or steady me when I
would have rushed in to give my parental "wisdom."

Let us look once again at this multidimensional story to
learn something more about our freedom. The story of the
prodigal is, in fact, about a man with two sons. It is the tale
of the younger son that gives this parable its title.

> The young man said to his father, "Father, I don't
> want to wait till you die. Give me the share of the
> property that will belong to me so I can do what I
> want." So the father divided his property between his
> two sons.
>
> The younger son gathered all he had and traveled
> to a distant country, and there he wasted his money.
> Soon it was all gone. When he had spent everything,
> a severe famine took place throughout that country.
> In desperation the young man went and found a job
> taking care of pigs. He lived with the pigs, ate with
> pigs, slept with pigs, and smelled like a pig! He was
> so hungry, even the slop the pigs ate looked good to
> him; and no one gave him anything.
>
> But then he came to himself: "My father's hired
> hands have more than enough to eat, but here I am
> dying of hunger! I will get up and go to my father,
> and I will say to him, 'Father, I am so sorry for what
> I have done and how I have hurt you; I am no longer

worthy to be called your son; treat me as one of your hired hands.'" So he headed for home.

While he was still far off, his father saw him. He ran to enfold his son in a warm embrace. Then the son said to him, "Father, I have made a mess of things. I have hurt you and I have squandered our wealth; I am no longer worthy to be called your son." But the father called to his servants, "Quickly, bring out a robe—the best one—and put it on him; put a ring on his finger and sandals on his feet. Let us have a party and celebrate; for this son of mine was dead and is alive again; he was lost and is found."

The breadth of God's forgiveness, the depth of God's love, and the grace to wait—true wisdom for parenting—are all displayed in this simple story.

The powerful powerlessness of parenting is akin to the self-imposed impotence of God in the face of our choices. Like the father in the parable, who just sits there day after day helpless—in a way—God is not willing to do anything to infringe upon our freedom. The father of the prodigal wants, he *really* wants, his son to come back, but he holds back from saying or doing anything that would thwart his son's freedom. In the parable we see the father's longing. We can imagine him stepping out of his house each day to sit where he can watch the long road. Then finally, one day, *waaaay* over *theeereee* in the distance he sees a figure approach. He recognizes the form, the gait of his son. He runs—he doesn't stand on ceremony or nurse his dignity—he runs to meet his child. Can't you just see it, the old man lifting his robes and racing helter-skelter across the fields?

Is there a parent who has not known some shade of the prodigal? Whether the tantrums of a toddler or the curious testing of a teenager, some aspect of the prodigal is an integral part of the parenting experience. Mpho, mothering her older daughter through teenage trials, knows the conundrum. She knows that she is not standing in the middle of her daughter's adolescent life. There are times, Mpho tells me, when she recognizes that her will for her daughter and what the child chooses to do will differ. She can tell her daughter the consequences of some of her decisions, but then it is the child who makes the choice.

A mother can exercise her limited power over her child in precisely the way God limits God's power over us. God is all-powerful, but this powerfulness is not the kind that sweeps away everything before it. In Christian theology God exercises God's power by being utterly vulnerable. God's power is the kind of power that waits, willing the prodigal to return. It is the kind of power that sets out to seek the lost sheep. It is the kind of power that offers itself even to death. It is the kind of power that dies.

God's regard for our freedom does not leave us to our own devices to muddle through our choices on our own. The shepherd of Luke's Gospel parable lets us see that God honors our choices yet seeks us out.

"Which one of you," Jesus asks, "having a hundred sheep and losing one of them, does not leave the ninety-nine in the wilderness and go after the one that is lost until he finds it?"

God is that shepherd who leaves ninety-nine sheep who have not been troublesome to go in search of the one that is lost. Can you believe it? He leaves ninety-nine perfectly good sheep, sheepish sheep, to go in search of one, and that one not intent on returning!

Biblical literature is peppered with prophets who call the people back to God. In this role they are like the shepherd seeking out the lost sheep. In our own time there are individuals and organizations that serve a similar function. The ones that call our attention to environmental degradation and global warming exercise something of the prophetic function. Peace activists and human-rights campaigners who tell us truths we know but try to forget also speak in the prophetic voice. The function of the prophets was not to forecast doom but to call us back to a better way of living. Their task was and is to call us back to wholeness. But it is still our choice.

We know the rightness of the prophet's call. We know the joy of doing what is right. We experience goodness as a feeling in our bones, but evil still tempts us. From Eve and the serpent to our own daily lives we are constantly confronted with the choice between right and wrong, and often wrong seems more attractive.

Wrong gratifies in the moment. The lie that gets us out of trouble in this instant often plagues us for hours or days to come. "Will I be found out?" we worry. "What other lie must I tell to make the first one stand?" we fret. The anxiety attached to the wrong may eventually make the fix seem worse than the ailment.

Sometimes the effects of choices are not felt in our own lifetime but will be felt in a future that we will not inhabit. Because of global warming and environmental degradation, the choices we make today will dictate the quality of life our grandchildren can enjoy.

Our choices, for good or ill, are habits of mind and action. The kindergartner whose disruptive antics win attention can become the coworker who compromises productivity with practical jokes. That person enjoys a moment of gratification but the in the long term may experience shunning. Making good choices is different. The teenager whose stylish flair is noted and encouraged may become the designer everyone wants to wear. The habit of fostering her own creativity can yield a lifetime of fulfilling work for the designer.

Though wrong gratifies in the moment, good yields its gifts over a lifetime. Each time we choose good, we add to the human treasury of goodness. Whether we make choices for ourselves and our personal health or we make choices for our family, community, and planet, we can choose good.

We know this even if we do not always practice it. We know that there are long-term health benefits to exercise. Each day we can choose whether or not we engage in it. We know that our families need both "quality time" and a substantial "quantity" of our time and attention to flourish. Every day we can choose whether and how we meet those needs. When we step out into our neighborhoods, we can engage in the practices of good neighborliness or we can choose not to. The quality of life on our planet now and in the future will be determined by the small daily choices that we make as much as by the big decisions in the corridors of power. Gandhi proclaimed that we must "be the change we want to see." The disciplines of most religions are designed to support us in choosing good. The world we want will dictate the choices we make.

How can we inculcate the practice of choosing good? We can pattern ourselves on people who have developed the practice. There are people who seem to select the good even when it seems not to serve their best interests.

When I chaired South Africa's Truth and Reconciliation Commission, I heard tales of many atrocities committed by human beings against other human beings. In each story of torture and pain there was also a story of incredible courage. What was particularly striking to me were the many, many testimonies by perpetrators about the people they had imprisoned, tortured, and killed. The wrongdoers were stunned by the courage of their victims. They noted the conviction that made South African martyrs stand firm in the face of certain death and uncertain repute. These people endured torture, and some went to their deaths, believing that freedom would come. They believed that by their lives and by their deaths they would have contributed to that freedom. They went to their deaths not knowing that anyone would tell the tale of their valor but being courageous nonetheless.

One such person was Phila Portia Ndwandwe. Phila Ndwandwe was a nursing mother and the commander of the MK in Swaziland. In October 1988 the Port Natal branch of the notorious South African security police kidnapped her.

After she disappeared it was suspected that she had defected to the other side, that she had become an informer for the security police, a collaborator, and that she was hidden in their protection. The Truth and Reconciliation Commission uncovered the facts of her disappearance.

She was kidnapped from her base in Swaziland and transported back over the border to South Africa. For ten days her kidnappers kept her naked in a closed room on Elandskop Farm in KwaZulu-Natal. In that time she was interrogated, assaulted, and tortured. Her captors wanted to make her reveal the plans of her unit. She maintained her silence. "I would rather die," she told them. On the tenth day she formed a pair of panties for herself from a blue plastic bag, a piece of rubbish she found lying around. It is testimony to the respect that her captors had developed for her that they did not strip her again before they executed her.

Two of her captors dug a pit and made her kneel on the ground at its edge. She was shot in the back of the head, execution style, and buried. When her body was exhumed by her killers, her skeleton was recognized by the blue plastic bag that still clung to her pelvic bones. "God, but she was brave," one of her murderers testified.

Ten years after her death the truth of her tale was told and the young boy who had been her infant son could claim his mother as a hero of South Africa's struggle. Phila chose to do what was right though it was costly to her and costly to her family. She had no guarantee that the truth of her fearlessness would ever be known by any except the men who killed her. The reality was that, for many years, her family was subjected to persistent rumors of her defection. But Phila had grasped a deeper truth: opting for the easy wrong may save the body, but it kills the soul. Life is more than breath and a heartbeat; meaning and purpose are the life of life. When we recognize that our lives have meaning beyond our cares and comforts, we tap the source of true joy.

Choosing good regardless of the consequences isn't the province only of freedom fighters. Choices and their consequences confront us every day. Recently my godson, Desmond, was robbed. He was standing with a friend outside a fast-food store. A group of boys accosted his friend and began to manhandle him. Desmond sprang to his friend's aid, joining the fray. Desmond and his friend got the worst of it. They were robbed of jackets, shoes, cell phones, and iPods. When Desmond told her what had happened, his mother threw up her hands, uncertain how to respond. "I wanted to scream at him, 'You could have been killed!' But I know that if he had left his friend to fend for himself, something essential about my Desmond would have died." Life is more than breath and a heartbeat.

As pastors, Mpho and I find one of our roles to be midwives of meaning. We guide those in our care to discern a purpose in their challenges, in their suffering, and in their joy. We help people to construct a life that they can inhabit from the mosaic tiles of their experience. The logic of Christian faith—indeed, the logic of *ubuntu*—is that our lives are not all about us. In the deepest, most significant way, the goal of human life is not to wring the greatest personal pleasure out of every moment. The goal of human life is to live beyond the small, narrow prison of our own cares, wants, and worries. By learning to choose what is good and right, we give ourselves the keys to true freedom.

Choosing to do what is good becomes a habit. Like all habits, it can be learned and fostered. When our children were young, a visit to their grandmother's house often included a meal served on a common plate. The younger girls and their cousin would sit on the polished red veranda outside the front door sharing a plate of pap (cornmeal mush) and *wors* (spicy beef sausage). It was the task of the older children to make sure that the smaller ones had enough to eat. The lessons of learning to look beyond your own immediate interests started early and were reinforced in ways large and small.

We tease my oldest daughter, Thandi. Although her nuclear family is small, she always cooks as though preparing to feed the biblical five thousand. I smile because this trait reminds me of my mother, who, even when we were at our poorest, always made enough to feed several unexpected guests. This habit of generosity was not one that was overtly taught, but it is one that I hope has been well learned.

My mother didn't reprimand me when as a teenager I returned from the Johannesburg station one sweater poorer. It was so cold that day that I had been wearing two sweaters because I didn't own a coat. As I hurried through the crowded station, my mind bent on the coal fire in the kitchen at home, I saw a boy shivering in the biting wind that whipped around the pillars. I motioned him toward me, and we huddled in a corner while I stripped off my outer layer and gave it to him. Though the air was frigid, the glow of his grateful smile warmed me as I raced the rest of the way home.

As I grew into adulthood I learned from the enduring example of my mother's generosity. The habit of hospitality was reinforced by the experience of Leah's gift. I learned a deep reverence for and delight in all humanity from my friend and mentor Trevor Huddleston. The people whom I loved and admired reinforced the habit of choosing what is good and right above what is comfortable or expedient in me. In later years I attended St. Peter's Seminary. There the Brothers of the Community of the Resurrection taught me. Their academic teaching was matchless, but it was their example that showed me the liberating gift of a friendship with God.

At the seminary we had what was called "recreation," meaning physical work. Early on it became my job to clean the community chapel, the brothers' chapel. In those years the brothers spent six or seven hours each day in corporate prayer. Even so there was never a time that I went into that sanctuary, early or late, that I did not find one of the brothers sitting in that silent space huddled in his cloak, deep in prayer. It was from the brothers that I learned the habit of prayer. My own prayer has been the staff that supported me during the darkest periods of our history. In prayer I have been challenged or chided. In prayer I have been comforted.

Because I treasure the friendship with God that has developed in those times of prayer, the habit of choosing right has been reinforced. In any loving relationship there are two approaches to making the right decision. One can make the right decision out of fear—to stave off the beloved's anger—or one can make the right decision to inspire the beloved's delight. When we are truly free we act out of the impulse to delight, not out of the fear of falling out of favor. When love is the motivation, the habit of choosing right becomes ingrained. It is etched into our being. When love is the motivation for choosing what is good and right, then what is wrong, no matter how expedient, is repellent.

We can inculcate the habit of choosing good. We can teach it to our children and to those in our charge. When our children were young, Leah and I placed a high premium on honesty. So the child who broke a treasured vase and came to confess her carelessness received no reprimand. We expressed our upset but thanked her for her honesty.

As adults we can also cultivate the practice of choosing right. We can foster it in ourselves. The Christian Gospels have a series of passages that enjoin the reader to "keep awake." Modern culture would prefer that we move through life half asleep. We are encouraged to make selections by default, not by conscious choice. So sometimes we do not actively opt to do wrong. But because we don't actively choose to do what is right, we slip into wrongness. The practices of goodness are practices of vigilance and conscious choice. They are habits of self-knowledge.

Self-knowledge supports the practices of goodness. When we are well acquainted with our gifts and our deficits, we know the challenges to goodness that require our extra vigilance. We know when our desire for goodness requires extra support. Choosing what is good and right is not intended to be a solitary journey. We can look to God to support our choices. We can look to friends or other guides to help us along the way.

Choosing what is good and right is a practice that can be learned. But as we will see in the next chapter, we can also slide down the slope of misdeeds into the habits of wrongness. I will begin by telling you about two encounters from my childhood that underscore this point.

But first turn with us into the stillness and listen to God speak with the voice of the heart:

I hear your frantic pounding at the doors of heaven.
All the furies of hell are snapping at your heels.
All your fears and desires screaming through the darkness.
The goodness you would choose is slipping away
And the wrong seems ever closer at hand.

Dear one, I have not hidden myself in heaven,
I am hidden in your heart.

I will not roar above the noise of your desires.
I will not drown out the clangor of your schemes.
Will you listen if I shout louder than the demons?
Will you know my voice if I scream?

No, child, listen for my whisper.
You are free to make that choice.
You are free to run from the whirlwind.
You are free to set out and seek out peace.

Leave lies alone,
They are a prison
In which you are endlessly tortured by your own voice.
The violence you commit throws up walls of anger and alienation
*   around you.*
Each cruelty is a thorn in the thicket that obscures your beauty.
Each kindness offered and each word of truth spoken
Is another key to break you free.

I have not hidden myself in heaven.
I have not shut my eyes or closed my ears.
I see that mother crying. I hold her through her slow hot tears.
Her wandering son is my child too.
We watch together when he chooses what is bad and wrong
Though we showed him what is good and right.
I am waiting with that helpless father.
We watch his daughter's teenage sulky rage.
"Patience," he may hear me whisper,
"She'll come back, she loves you so."
"She doesn't know how to be who she is
or who she is becoming."

Child, I hear you sighing, sobbing.
I see your shoulders slumping in defeat,
Always trying, often failing, the right you do seems to turn out
*   wrong.*

My precious child,
I will call you to account for nothing more than I have asked of you.
Just be faithful to the task I have set before you.
Whether you succeed or not is no matter to me.
Live as you hear me speak in you.
Live the truth you learn from me.
Then it doesn't matter how the road may turn.
The goodness you live will set you free.

5

THE HABITS OF WRONGNESS

Pik swart!" ("black pick!"), I heard them shout as my legs pumped furiously on the bicycle pedals. I was panting and sweating as I sped past the group of sneering white boys. I was afraid of that mocking little gang, but I was also angry. In a few moments I was far enough away that I judged they couldn't catch me. Only then, heart racing, did I spin around to face them. "*Graf!*" ("Shovel!"), I yelled, my clever retort. I knew from their tone that they had insulted me. But I hadn't understood the insult: not a "black pick," a tool to break up hard ground, but "pitch black." They learned them so early, these insults of racism. The words of disdain that adults offered at the dinner table were repeated in the sneering taunts heard on the street. I ran that gauntlet so many times as a boy. In the black township outside Ventersdorp, where I grew up, for a long time I was the only boy who had a bicycle. On most days my father would send me the few miles to the white town to buy his tobacco or the newspaper. Each trip would include the hostile meeting with that little troop.

The taunts of racism were learned early. They didn't come naturally. They were learned. The painful effects of racism were felt early too. I remember as a young boy being sent into town on a weekday. Classes had already started, but my father wanted something or other from the store. I went past the white children's school and saw black children from our township scavenging in the dustbins. The government had a school-based food program for white children, but those children would throw that bread and fruit in the trash because they preferred the food their mommies sent with them. There was no meal program for black children. Their mommies often couldn't afford to buy them bread, fruit, or anything else to eat. There had been a government food program for black children, too, but when the Nationalist Party—the architects of apartheid—came into power, they abolished the program. "We can't provide for all the black children," Prime Minister Hendrik Verwoerd explained, "so we won't provide for any of them." As children, black or white, we learned not to challenge the illogical logic of racist practices and assumptions.

The effects of racism were first felt early in life and were experienced until death. The insults of racism, once learned, were employed daily. Sometimes the humiliations were small, seemingly insignificant things. I remember going into a shop with my father. He was the principal of the elementary school and a leading figure in the black community. I must have been about six at the time. I was so proud of my tall, handsome, educated dad. The person behind the counter, a little slip of a white girl, barely even a teenager, called out to him, "*Ja*, boy?" She was only living what she had learned— disrespect for an elder of a different race.

I wondered how he was feeling to be so demeaned in front of his child. Years later I sampled that humiliation. Our family was newly returned from England, and I was in Port Elizabeth with Mpho. We walked past a playground. It was full of children enjoying the warm sunshine, playing on the swings and slides. Mpho wanted to go and join in the play. I didn't have the words to explain to my three-year-old daughter that she was not like those children. The park was for whites only.

Apartheid was instituted as a sweeping set of laws and regulations that determined every aspect of a person's life on the basis of their race. It was experienced as a series of daily injustices and humiliations against people of color that stoked the anger of black people and dulled the sensibilities of white people. In isolation, each of the incidents I described earlier was a small thing. But these hurts and hardships that white South Africans inflicted on their black compatriots were part of a process that got white people used to dehumanizing black people.

Learning racism had to be a process. It wasn't an instinct. Racism is evil, and evil goes against the grain of creation. Because we are made for goodness, the instinct to do what is right must be eroded to allow us to do what is wrong. The people who codified and instituted the apartheid system recognized that reality. They understood the importance of the details of dehumanizing: separate doors, different amenities, exclusive beaches and benches.

They knew that the mechanics mattered. For example, the pass books that everyone had to carry and that black people so hated. The document detailed the pass holder's age, race, and gender. The book then went on to record the owner's driving record, record of employment, and marital status. For black people a series of endorsements detailed where they could live and where they were eligible to seek employment. These details made the pass book an effective tool to control the movements of black people. The book treated black South Africans like aliens in the land of their birth.

The minutiae of segregation mattered. Separate and unequal schools, different neighborhoods, and the hierarchy of services were all created with due deliberation. Each privilege adopted without question made the next privilege seem more like an entitlement. With each assent the instinct for right was further eroded. With each assent the habit of choosing wrong was learned and ingrained.

If we are made for goodness, where does wrong come from? The ancients had thought long and hard about just this question. The authors of the biblical creation stories took it as given that the good God had created all that is to be good. They also took it as given that freedom of choice was one attribute with which the creator had endowed human beings. They had studied human nature. They understood that evil takes root by a series of small decisions. So they explained the advent of wrong in creation by telling the tale of a succession of seemingly insignificant choices—the story of Adam, Eve, the serpent, and the forbidden fruit. In the book of Genesis God planted a garden in Eden. In that paradise first man and first woman made their home. Everything in Eden was perfect.

Did I say everything was perfect? It was not quite so. Among the inhabitants of Eden was a serpent. The serpent was a wily creature and ready to tempt the human to stray.

"Eve," he called, in a gentle, wheedling tone, "Eve, was there anything in the garden that God said you may not have?"

"'You shall not eat of the fruit of the tree that is in the middle of the garden, nor shall you touch it, or you shall die,'" reported Eve.

"Oh, you won't die!" responded the snake, managing to sound both amused and exasperated. "God wouldn't kill you! Here, try this. It's amazing. It tastes delicious, and when you eat it you'll become as wise as God. You will know good and evil."

"Really?" Eve asked, curiosity and excitement at war with her instinctive desire to abide by the rules. Curiosity and excitement won. She ate the fruit. She gave some to her husband, who also ate.

And so it began: the first drip of depravity entered creation with the serpent's temptation and the human's consent.

"Then the eyes of both were opened, and they knew that they were naked; and they sewed fig leaves together and made loincloths for themselves.

"They heard the sound of the Lord God walking in the garden at the time of the evening breeze,"

"Uh-oh, it's God. Hide!" So the man and woman hid among the trees.

But God called to them, "Where are you?"

Adam answered, "I heard the sound of you walking in the garden, and I was afraid, because I was naked; and I hid myself."

"Who told you that you were naked? Have you eaten from the tree of which I commanded you not to eat?"

Like every miscreant after him, Adam tries to minimize his own responsibility by shifting the blame. His first target is God; then he fingers Eve.

"The woman whom *you* gave to be with me, *she* gave me fruit from the tree, and I ate."

Then God said to the woman, "What have you done?"

In like manner, Eve shoves the blame onto the snake: "The serpent tricked me and I ate."

Adam and Eve may have been the first to engage in rationalizations and half-truths, but they were not the last. In biblical literature what began with the snake in Eden was the germ that infected all creation and became epidemic. Evil proliferated until murder and mayhem became the order of the day.

A cursory glance at the last century of human history echoes the biblical progress of wrong. The wholesale slaughters that were hallmarks of the Rwandan genocide and the Nazi holocaust were not sudden events. The horrors of apartheid did not spring from nothing into full bloom. In each case the path from goodness to evil was laid carefully. In order to permit ourselves to inflict wanton harm, our actions must be accompanied by a host of rationalizations and justifications.

Those we call national enemies are described first as "them" and then in progressively less human terms before the bombing can start. The rhetoric of the Nazis, the propaganda of the apartheid government, the voices of those who stoked the fury of the Rwandan genocide—in example after example throughout history the drums of war have been preceded by caricatures of those on the other side. First they are described as different. Then details of difference are used to establish them as "less than" or "worse than" us. Then they are likened to animals. Later they are called beasts. Finally they are vermin to be destroyed. Wrong is clearly against the grain of creation. Were it not so, the wrong we do would need no explanation.

In the Bible, depravity does not enter creation in a tidal wave of wrongness. It comes in as a slow, silent leak, drip by quiet drip, until the earth is flooded. This was true of the biblical history. It is true in world history. It holds true for our own lives. We do not veer off the rails in an explosion of error. We make a succession of uncorrected missteps, and then when we check, the good we would do seems far out of reach. Our media report the dramatic end. The public learns the truth when the deed is done. What we seldom learn are the small acts of misrepresentation that paved the way for the larger lies. The padded expense reports, the feigned illness, the willfully inaccurate account of one's movements, the titillating half-truths about other people—these are also part of the story. Each on its own is not an act of wanton perversion. Each opens the door for the next wrong; each sets the stage for the cascade of corruption.

It is for just this reason that many Rules of Life include a commitment to a daily examination of conscience. A Rule of Life is the set of disciplines by which members of a religious community agree to abide. The simple question "Where was God in this?" can throw one's behavior into stark relief. Mpho invites her children to examine their interactions with two questions: "Was it nice?" and "Was it necessary?" Those two questions can serve adults as well as they serve children.

We are going to make mistakes. Sometimes our actions and utterances are neither nice nor are they necessary. The purpose of the questions is not to drive us into shame or guilt. Shame and guilt only pave the way to excuses, rationalizations, and justifications. They open the door to more cruelty. Rather, the questions "Was it nice?" and "If it wasn't nice, was it necessary?" let us recognize the harm we have inflicted while the hurt is still fresh enough to assuage.

The once-popular message "Love means never having to say, 'I'm sorry'" is quite wrong. Love means daring to say, "I'm sorry." In fact, given who we are, love means saying "I'm sorry" early and often. Mpho's husband, Joe, is a sturdy tower of a man. Mpho tells him he is never manlier than when he crouches down to apologize to one of his children for an unjust reprimand or an excess of temper. Apology and forgiveness break the hold of wrongness. Self-forgiveness may be the golden key that frees us from slipping into the habit of choosing wrong.

Sometimes it does not take a formal examination of conscience to halt one in one's tracks. A question, a comment, or an observation can be all it takes to make one turn aside from a slide into wrong. Mpho told me about an encounter during her time in Grahamstown that alerted her to her own casual wastefulness.

Grahamstown is a city in the Eastern Cape, the poorest of South Africa's nine provinces. The unemployment rate hovers around 22 percent in the province. In Rhini, the black township that clings to the hills surrounding the city, the unemployment rate may be as high as 50 percent. Many of those who do have jobs are underemployed or underpaid.

With a husband earning an American salary, a grant for work she was engaged in, and a favorable exchange rate, by Grahamstown standards Mpho was rich. Each day a woman from Rhini would come to clean the house, bake bread, and manage the family's laundry. She was paid something more than the going rate for her labor and was provided with breakfast and lunch.

Mpho likes to keep fresh fruit in a bowl on the dining-room table in her home, and South Africa is a wonderful place for a fruit lover. There are peaches and plums, apples and grapes, lychees, oranges, mangoes, bananas, and melons of every kind in their seasons. In the Eastern Cape there are also the sweet prickly pears. The fruit bowl looked like a cornucopia. Occasionally the fruit wouldn't be eaten in time and one piece would spoil in the bowl. Mpho would throw this item in the trash so that the rot would not infect the rest of the bowl. One day the housekeeper came to Mpho with a peach from the trashcan. "Do you mind if I have this?" she asked. "It's only got this one spot. I can cut that away and eat the rest."

Discarding a piece of partially rotten fruit was not an act of wanton depravity. At home in Virginia or even in produce-rich Cape Town it is almost a housewifely act to toss a piece of rotting fruit into the trash. It ensures that the rest of the bowl stays fresh and whole. In the poverty of Grahamstown, where adults beg for daily bread and children go hungry, it was a single instance of the kind of mindlessness that daily disciplines of recollection are designed to halt.

When she was growing up, Mpho would say she couldn't understand the logic of eating all the food on her dinner plate in London because children were starving in Biafra. "Send *them* my dinner. I don't want it." Face-to-face with a want that would pull a peach from her garbage taught her the habit of thought that gratefully appreci-ates the abundance of all that she has. Perhaps a child in Biafra was too far away to make the point about hunger and having. In Grahamstown, the fact of hunger had a familiar face and a known name.

The practices of goodness—noticing, savoring, think-ing, enjoying, and being thankful—are not hard disciplines to learn. But they *are* disciplines, and they take practice.

The habits that allow wrong to become entrenched—mindlessness or tuning out, inattentiveness, the busyness of doing to distraction, and an ungrateful heart—can take hold so easily.

Each habit that allows wrong to become entrenched feeds from the others. Our lives are busy and active. There is barely a moment to rest. Doing feeds the distraction that makes us inattentive. When we carve out time to really rest and be restored, we also restore our ability to be attentive.

Recently Mpho shared a stage with my dear friend and spiritual brother the Dalai Lama. She told me that the man accompanying His Holiness, his translator, Thupten Jinpa, struck her by the quality of his attention. Through a long morning of presentations and discussions Dr. Jinpa listened carefully, ready to translate a word or a concept from English to Tibetan or from Tibetan to English for His Holiness. What Mpho noticed was that Dr. Jinpa could not allow his attention to flag, even for a moment. At any instant His Holiness might not have access to the English word that explained his thought. He might not understand the English explanation of another person's ideas. Mpho reflected that the intense listening necessary for one to serve as a simultaneous translator was similar to the deep listening required of a spiritual director. Her spiritual direction practice must be supported by periods of deep rest.

Tuning out is not rest. "Zoning out" is not restorative. When we tune out, we pretend to pay attention when in fact our minds have wandered away. Often the person who has sought our attention notices that we are not really listening to him and so feels cheated in the encounter. We, in our turn, may feel guilty or resentful. Neither of those emotions secures for us the respite our tuning out was meant to provide.

"Zoning out"—an activity usually accomplished with the aid of a television set—does not reinvigorate us. There is brainwork involved in struggling with the mixed message: The television offers input, but we are mentally exhausted. Is our brain meant to engage with the input? If our minds are not expected to engage with the material, our frazzled brains might ask, why is it being presented? Why not turn off the device and rest? "Zoning out" and the mixed message it creates reinforce the idea that we are "supposed to be doing something." That idea can be the source of so much guilt and resentment. We "zone out" though we want to rest. But we are afraid to really rest because we are supposed to be doing something. The worry and resentment that accompany the mixed message are not food for a grateful heart.

We answer our worry with entitlement and ingratitude: "I am busy, tired, and stressed, so I am entitled to a respite. I will zone out in front of the television." And we continue to be tired, busy, and stressed.

Real respite and restoration foster gratitude. When we allow ourselves to really rest, we can be thankful for the blessing of honest fatigue. When we experience full restoration we have the energy to honestly enjoy—to think and to savor. Rest and rejuvenation allow us to really pay attention. And this attention is a key discipline for the practices of goodness.

When hardships befall us, we cry out to heaven, "Why me?" When good fortune attends us, it is the grateful heart that has the courage to ask, "Why me?" The Buddhist practice of mindfulness and the daily *examen* of Ignatian spirituality point to the same end: when we pay attention, it is possible to halt evil in its tracks. Paying attention also helps us to see how easy it is to become inured to the proliferation of evil. Evil does not sweep in like a tsunami; it bleeds into the fabric of life, washing out the joy and staining the beauty.

Choosing wrong is learned through a series of small decisions. Little failures become ingrained through repetition. The small faults, unchecked, open the way for all the vileness of which we are capable. In the next chapter we will see that suffering is part of the human condition. Sometimes we create our own suffering. Sometimes suffering comes unbidden, caused by others. I will recount the story of one community that endured decades of suffering.

But first turn with us into the stillness and listen to God speak with the voice of the heart:

I hear your call as you are falling.
You stumble over your own wrongdoing and topple into the
    bottomless pit of guilt and shame.
But there is no abyss. It is an illusion.
There is no depth to which you can fall that is beyond my reach.
I have lived with you from the age of the ages.
The dream of you has delighted me; the fact of you pleases me.
There is a choice in every moment.

In every moment there is a chance to flourish and not to fail.

Every instant is rich with possibility.

I have not carved out the path that you must follow; we form the way together, you and I.

I have destined you for good and a field of goodness lies before you.

Listen to me, and though the way may not be easy, every step and stone will lead to joy.

Turn aside to heed the voice of the tempter and faltering will mark your journey.

I trust you, my child.

Even when you have fallen the road does not end.

You can rise up from the ground and turn around.

You can repent and head for your home in me.

Seek me out.

You will find me.

I have been here from eternity.

Until eternity this is where I will be.

I am waiting and you will find me.

6

WHERE IS GOD WHEN WE SUFFER?

We felt battle weary. We had spent the night outside, keeping vigil on the hillside above Mogopa. For months we had waged a court battle with the apartheid authorities. Now, as we huddled together, breath misting in the predawn air, it was hard to hold on to our defiance. It all seemed so pointless. The place where we stood had so recently been a thriving community. The evidence was in the rubble all around us. More than four hundred families had lived here. In the seventy years since the Bakwena people had bought this land, they had worked hard to establish their village. They had hewn stone from the surrounding hills for their buildings. Three hundred and thirty houses had dotted this hillside. There had been a high school, a primary school, several stores, and four churches. The community even boasted a clinic. The village of Mogopa also had several boreholes and a reservoir—important assets in this drought-prone region. But Mogopa was what the apartheid government called a "black spot"—an area inhabited by black people surrounded by white communities. A blight on the segregationists' grand design.

History didn't matter. The Bakwena had come to this area outside Ventersdorp in 1913. They were victims of the Native Land Act, one of the legal machinations essential to the establishment of the apartheid system. This law designated 10 percent of South Africa's landmass for black habitation. It also made it illegal for black South Africans to continue to live and graze their cattle on white-owned farms as sharecroppers or tenant farmers. The act had the desired effects, and they were devastating. Hundreds of thousands of people lost their homes and their livelihoods.

Forcibly removed from the land, with nowhere to graze their cattle, black people became part of a pool of cheap labor available to enhance white wealth. The Bakwena sold their cattle to finance the purchase of two adjoining farms. They believed they had escaped from being forced to work for white South Africans. They thought that they had secured a different future than perpetual servitude for themselves and their descendants. They thought that with the land purchase they had bought a measure of self-determination.

But Mogopa was a "black spot," and by the late 1960s

the apartheid government had determined that it must be erased. So began a series of legal maneuvers by the government. The efforts to evict the Bakwena were complicated by the fact that the Bakwena held title to the property they inhabited.

In 1983 the government decided to persuade the community to move "voluntarily." They terminated the bus service between Mogopa and the nearby town of Ventersdorp. They withdrew the teachers from the primary and high schools. They demolished the school buildings. They bulldozed the churches. They destroyed the clinic. They removed the pumps that supplied the village with water. By August 1983, 170 families had given up and left. The government razed their houses. They parked a bulldozer in the village and knocked down the houses of people who left the village for any reason. On August 21, 1983, the government issued a "Removal Order" that stated that the remaining members of the community must leave within ten days or be forcibly removed. An interdict to stop the removal and leave to appeal the ruling were denied.

It was ten days later that our slightly dispirited group held this all-night vigil in Mogopa. We sang songs and stamped our feet against the cold. It felt like a gathering of the usual suspects, stalwarts of the antiapartheid struggle. There were some of the indomitable women of the Black Sash—white women with the courage to stand for justice; many of the members of my staff at the South African Council of Churches were there; Alan Boesak of the World Congress of Reformed Churches and members of the United Democratic Front stood with us. Where, I wondered, was God?

An old man, a villager, stood up to pray: "God, we know you are with us. We thank you for loving us." His words surprised me. Where was the evidence of God's presence? What did God's love matter against the grim inevitability of the bulldozers and the apartheid machine?

The demolition crew did not come that day. Perhaps the crowd deterred them. Emboldened by the government inaction in the months that followed, the community rebuilt some of their houses. They reestablished the bus line and restored the schools. Then, without warning, on Valentine's Day 1984 the police moved in. They cordoned off the area and cut off the telephone lines. In one day the remaining 350 families were forcibly relocated to the nominally independent Bophuthatswana homeland.

Once again it seemed that evil had triumphed. The Bakwena ba Mogopa were hauled from their land and dumped, like so much garbage, in a desolate place far from the farms that they had made home. How could God allow this to happen? Why did God stand by while a community was swallowed by this violation of justice? Seeing the courage, determination, and dignity of those villagers, why did God let callousness reign? Did God even see their suffering? Had God fallen asleep or, perhaps, just gone away? I joined my angry lament with the psalmist's cry and the plea of oppressed people through the ages:

Rouse yourself! Why do you sleep, O God?
Awake, do not cast us off forever!
Why do you hide your face?
Why do you forget our affliction and oppression? (Ps. 44:23–24)

When we have done what is good, just, and right and our best efforts are met with failure, it is easy to doubt the presence of God. We couldn't stop the apartheid machine in that moment. Year followed year, and the dehumanizing segregationists ruled our lives. We knew evil. Evil makes a child of God doubt that he or she is a child of God. In this place evil seemed always to hold the winning hand.

The questions that injustice forced us to wrestle with are the same questions that have plagued human beings for generations and that beset us even now. Is God omnipresent? If God is everywhere, why is there no evidence of God's presence when we are suffering now and here? Is God omnipotent? If God is all-powerful, why do we suffer? Is God really good? How can a good God allow evil a place in creation? How can an omnipotent God be so impotent in the face of injustice? What does omnipresence matter if God sees but does not relieve our pain? The answers we have to these questions are not complete, nor do they rest easy with us.

But the old man in Mogopa was right: God is omnipresent. God is with us in the muck of our lives. Fear, suffering, and grief may obscure our vision of God. Sometimes we shut our eyes so tight against the pain that we can see no shaft of light. We can have no glimpse of God. But God is there. God stands with us in everything that we experience and endure.

If God is with us, and God is good, how can God watch while we suffer? Why does God not intervene to stir up the repentance of those who do us harm? Why does God not turn them aside from their wickedness? Because God is omniscient, omnipotent, and omnipresent, but God is not capricious. A God who would suspend the laws of nature may soothe us in one moment but would, ever after, upend our sense of safety. We could never rely on season following season. We could not be certain that heavy things would stay down or light things float up. A capricious God could, at any moment, decide that order had no place in creation.

God is consistent. The God who waits for us is the same God who waits for all humanity. As human beings we are prepared for God to wait for our repentance when we do wrong and are in need of forgiveness. The story of the prodigal son and his loving father is a source of comfort when we are the ones who have sinned, when we are the ones in the role of prodigal. We want the freedom to wander and the knowledge that we can return home to God. It is harder to accept God's reverence for human autonomy when we are the victims. It is harder to accept God's respect for human freedom when we must look with the God's-eye view.

When we must stand beside the father of the prodigal, trusting that his son will come to his senses and return home, the parable may not be so comforting. So many of us know the role of the prodigal's parent only too intimately. How many parents have had to wait through years of anguish for a child to kick a drug habit or win the battle with the bottle? How many were able to sit on their hands and watch their child flail like one drowning? How many parents could resist making the futile attempts to rescue their child? Being the parent of the prodigal is so different from being the prodigal child.

The example of God's loving patience is no easier to emulate when we are the injured party. The infinitely forgiving God is a balm to us when we have faltered or failed. The same God is a challenge to us when we have suffered mental anguish and physical harm. The God who waits for the human change of heart is cold comfort to the victims of human brutality. But God does not have a double standard. That God is consistent as an answer to the eternal questions of God's love and God's presence really does not rest easy with us.

It can be almost impossible to look at the perpetrators of evil with a God's-eye view. It seems unrealistic to expect those on the receiving end of grief, pain, and even death to trust that there is a spark of goodness in the people who hurt them. We are surprised and moved by the survivors of torture or the victims of abuse who do not thirst for revenge. We think that they must be made of different stuff than are we. Yet we do all have this capacity for compassion, even if in differing degrees. The ability to forgive even the smallest wrong depends, in part, on the belief that the perpetrator can act differently. Somewhere in our secret hearts we do in fact trust that this is a moral universe. Even if, in the moment, the power of goodness is invisible, we do trust that it exists.

It is a moral universe. We can trust that it is a moral universe because history bears out this assertion. Yes, each generation has its share of dictators and despots, but each generation also sees the demise of tyrants and the overthrow of autocratic governments that seemed invincible. We may not see the outcome of the struggles for justice and peace in our lifetime. The crisis in Darfur, the dictatorship in Burma, and the excesses of the Taliban may continue to be a part of our human story for years to come. But they will not continue forever. After all, who would have predicted the end of the Soviet Union, the birth of Namibia, peace in Northern Ireland, or the dawn of democracy in South Africa? These are changes that have occurred in living memory. As Dr. Martin Luther King Jr. observed, "The arc of the universe is long but it bends towards justice."

Waiting for justice to be established is a challenge to us. It confounds our sense of how God is supposed to act. When our prayers for right to prevail seem to go unanswered, we may become angry with God; we may doubt God's goodness, God's presence, or the very existence of God. But it is this seeming silence that assures us that God is not capricious. If God were to intervene at our command, the regularity of nature would disappear. Life would become a cartoonlike contest as each person waged a kind of prayer warfare for control of the power of God. It is in sometimes having our desires thwarted and our gratification denied or delayed that we recognize that we are not simply objects to be shuffled around in God's grand game. The grace of unanswered prayers is the knowledge that we are subjects in the story of our own lives. We all have some creative authority in the course of history.

Sometimes our acts seem too small and solitary to divert the course of history. Our stand or our suffering may represent the proverbial drop in the bucket. But, as Mpho likes to point out, there is always one final drop that makes the bucket overflow. So the protests of the women of the Black Sash were a drop in the bucket. The Black Sash was an organization of white women who opposed apartheid. They circumvented the laws against gatherings and "riotous assemblies" by standing as solitary protesters against the excesses of the government. The witness of the Mothers of the Plaza de Mayo was a drop in the bucket. For over three decades these women whose children disappeared in Argentina's dirty war have come to the plaza each Thursday for a thirty-minute vigil. Each wears a white headscarf embroidered with the name of her missing child. When their protest began, the police told them they could not congregate and they could not stand in one place, so they walked around the plaza in pairs.

Each of us, in our own time and place, can offer our suffering as a drop in the bucket of human agency that reshapes the course of history.

The story of the villagers of Mogopa is one illustration of human agency in the course of history. It is a story of faith. It is also a confirmation that this is a moral universe. Evil may, indeed, hold sway for the moment, but evil does not have the last word.

The story of Mogopa continued to unfold over many hard years. But eventually that old man's faith was vindicated. Through the decade following the destruction of their village the people of Mogopa continued to petition to be allowed to return to their land. In 1994 the newly elected parliament of the postapartheid South Africa passed the Restitution of Land Rights Act. The Bakwena ba Mogopa were among the first communities to return home. The old man was right. God was with them in the heart of their ruined community. Their faith in God's loving presence gave the villagers courage to continue their fight even though for years their prayers seemed to go unanswered. The experience of the Bakwena was instrumental in prompting the parliamentary action. For themselves and for thousands of others who had been forcibly stripped of their land rights, the Bakwena ba Mogopa had a hand in writing a just history of South Africa.

The people of Mogopa could see beyond the immediacy of their concerns. They continued to petition the government because they believed that the injustice done to them mattered. They believed that achieving justice mattered, if not for them, then for the generations that would follow them. Their suffering had meaning. Even in the bleakest periods of their fight they knew they were struggling for a worthwhile prize. They were working to pass a treasure to the next generation.

Sometimes struggles seem wrapped in futility. Both Mpho and I have been pastors to people at the end of their lives. We have visited with patients in hospice care and with those who love them. Some people come to hospice in old age. Hospice allows them to die with some measure of comfort and dignity. Some people come to hospice relatively young, riddled with cancer or other diseases. They come when every treatment has been tried and has failed. They come having admitted their own mortality and wanting to claim whatever treasures are left to them in this life. For those who love them, their sickness, suffering, and death may seem senseless.

One couple in Mpho's ministry had found new love in late middle age. They shared a delight in each other and joy in the life that they were making together. When the wife took ill, the deterioration was very fast. She made her peace with sickness and death. He harangued heaven with his questions: "Why did she have to suffer?" "Why must she be in pain?" "Why did God allow us to find each other only to wrench us apart?" The question left unspoken was "Why did *he* have to suffer?" After all, when people we love are sick, we suffer with them. We endure the agony of not knowing the contours of their agony. We bear the pain of not being able to alleviate their pain.

Suffering is a part of the human condition. Suffering teaches us our limitations and our vulnerabilities. We can choose to let our suffering drive us into community as we recognize and share our common experience. But we can choose to allow the experience to drive us apart and isolate us from one another. The shame of victimhood can be the most isolating kind of suffering. Sexual violence, domestic abuse, and infection with HIV/AIDS bring with them experiences of suffering that have been so stigmatized that people struggling with their effects are often isolated in their suffering.

But in God's eyes there is no hierarchy of suffering. God does not stand aloof, judging us and parsing our pain. The cause of our suffering does not matter to God. God suffers with us. The source of our pain does not matter to God. God only wills our healing. God does not desire that we suffer. But if we offer our suffering to God, God will use it.

Even if our suffering does not seem ennobling, there are gifts hidden in suffering that can be redeemed only in the experience. The suffering that comes with sickness can feel particularly fruitless, especially for the people who watch. The person who ails can inspire with her stoicism or good humor. The people who wait and watch, fret and pray, have only their compassion to offer. Compassion, which literally means "suffering with," may feel like the most futile kind of suffering. It changes nothing. It holds no hope of changing anything. Yet to be compassionate is to see with a God's-eye view. Compassion teaches us to sit with the father of the prodigal knowing that the story might not end as we hoped. *Ubuntu* theology is an understanding of life that values community. *Ubuntu* affords us the ability to endure knowing that our suffering in this moment may not be redeemed in our lifetime. *Ubuntu* allows us to affirm Dame Julian of Norwich when she observes that, in the fullness of time, "all shall be well. . . . And all manner of things shall be well."

Even when suffering holds no gifts for its victims, in the spirit of *ubuntu*, it can yield gifts for the wider community. In 2009 I was awarded the Presidential Medal of Freedom by President Barack Obama. One of my corecipients was Nancy Goodman Brinker. Nancy's older sister, Susan Komen, died in 1980. No one who loved Susan could consider the failure of her breast-cancer treatment, her suffering, and her death a gift. The failed treatment was not a gift for her. It was not a gift for her family. But as a result of Susan's suffering, her sister, Nancy, created a foundation that has been a gift for many millions of people around the world. In the years since Susan died, the foundation that Nancy created in her memory, Susan G. Komen for the Cure, has raised money for breast-cancer research, education, and health services. The work of the organization has resulted in new treatment options and higher quality of life for breast-cancer survivors. The door to hope and life for millions of people around the world was opened by the failure of a medical treatment and the suffering and the death of one woman.

Whatever we suffer, the God who sees eternity stands with us in the heart of our suffering. Whether we suffer with the goal of a better life in mind or when we suffer in sympathy with others, God stands beside us. Even when our pain is of our own making, we are not left to endure it alone. Failure brings with it a particular kind of suffering. In the next chapter we will explore the trials and the treasures that failure can bring. I will begin by telling you about one of my own failures.

But first let us turn into the stillness and listen to God speak with the voice of the heart:

I have seen suffering make heroes of some of my children.
The strength with which they endure their pain is a shining example
    to all.
But sometimes, child, suffering is only suffering.

It seems gratuitous.
It feels meaningless.
It teaches nothing.
It brings no gifts.
It just is.
It just is and you feel alone,
Abandoned,
Forsaken.
You think I have gone
So you run.
Your mind skitters away from the hurt.
Your body shrinks away from the pain.
Your heart tries to shut itself against the suffering.
I see you run.
You don't believe that I am with you.
But I am there.
When you stop running from the pain
And turn to face it,
When you can step into the agony and let it be,
When you can turn to your own suffering and know its name,
Then you will see me.
You will see me in the heart of it with you.
It doesn't matter if your body is wracked by pain
Or your mind is spiraling through aches and anguish.
When you stop running you will see me.
I will not forsake you.
I cannot abandon you.
You are not alone.
I am with you.

7

WHERE IS GOD WHEN WE FAIL?

The second parish where I served after my ordination to the priesthood was St. Philip's Thokoza, near Alberton. St. Philip's was wonderful for our family. We finally had a house after living in a single-car garage in my first parish. Leah was teaching at a local primary school, so our finances were a little better too.

I was the curate in charge of St. Philip's. It was an outstation of St. Peter's Chains, Natalspruit. The rector of St. Peter's Chains, my supervisor, was a wonderful man, Archdeacon Voyi. He really gave me all the latitude I could want. He allowed me to run St. Philip's almost as though I were the rector. I came with all the enthusiasm of someone recently priested.

One of the things I instituted in the parish was a daily Eucharist and the office of Evensong. I divided the parish into two sections, and on Fridays, instead of holding worship in the church, we had our service in one section of the parish or the other. We chose a house that was central to that section, and I would celebrate the Eucharist there in the morning. In the afternoon I would go and visit the sick and homebound in the other section of the parish. It was all so beautifully organized. I really thought I was the cat's whiskers.

Two things happened in close succession. The first was that I experienced one of the most wonderful things that could happen to a priest. I had gone to give a sick Communion to one of my parishioners who was ill. He was a man I was visiting quite regularly. After this particular visit someone came to the house to say that very soon after I gave him Communion he died. I felt very good, maybe even a little cocky, about being such a good and faithful pastor.

Not long after this experience I had another that was very different. I had completed my regular Friday rounds and was asked to visit a parishioner in the section not scheduled for visits. I had been told that the old lady was not well. A visit would have been more than was strictly required of me, but it would have been no great inconvenience. Thokoza was not very big, and her home was not too far from where we lived. I could have gone. But it wasn't the week for pastoral visits in that section. I didn't go. I went home. A few days later, before I got around to visiting her, she died.

I came down with a real crash. I had fallen victim to my own presumptuousness. I had refused to yield my neat schedule to a real need. I had put my own small convenience above the needs of someone in my care. I had given in to my own laziness. And now there was no way to repair the damage. It was particularly painful for me, a pastor. I claimed to follow Jesus. Even in a rush to heal one man's daughter, didn't Jesus pause to heal and hear another person in need? Did Jesus not abandon his haste to attend to the woman with a flow of blood (Luke 8:40–56, Mark 5:21–43, Matt. 9:18–26)?

That failure was a very humbling experience. It helped to shape my ministry. It dragged me away from my pride in my own plans and schemes. Knocked to my knees, I had the opportunity to rethink my life and my way of working. My smart designs and I had been shoved off the throne at the center of my life. God had my attention.

The years since those incidents have been marked by successes and by failures, from the small dramas of family life to the more public actions on the world stage. Leah and I have parented our children through their teenage years and beyond. We endured the jealousies and the screaming matches, and the unsuitable suitors that our children brought into our home. We learned, in that time, how little we knew and how heavily we had to lean on the grace of God.

The work of South Africa's Truth and Reconciliation Commission is also behind me. In many ways that was a stellar success. I worked with an incredible and gifted team of people. We helped South Africa on the road to healing much of the anguish that apartheid had wrought. But we failed to draw white South Africans into full participation in our work. That is a source of sadness. I have been able to endure the failures and maintain some humility in spite of the successes because of what happened in Thokoza. One legacy of the time in Thokoza has been the prayerful listening that has become so central a part of my ministry and my life.

To some of us the humiliation of failure seems to open a wide gulf between God and us. We imagine that God turns away from us in disgust. What I discovered was that failure could be a bridge across the chasm that pride had created. As long as I considered myself and my plans to be of paramount importance, I circumscribed the arena for God's action. In fact, my neat schedule and orderly life left little space for anyone to educate or influence me. That failure in Thokoza was a gift to me and to my ministry.

A failure can also be a gift when we have allowed ourselves the delusion that we are self-made. One of the enduring fictions of our time is that of the "self-made millionaire." The failures on the road to achieving the dream of wealth may be the windows through which self-aggrandizement can be ushered out to open a space for God. When we imagine we are self-made, we confine God to a controllable corner of our lives. After all, if we are self-made, then we are in charge. We know how our lives are meant to look and how to make them look that way. Failure offers us a chance to discern the hand of God in the pattern of our lives. It offers us the opportunity to acknowledge the contributions of so many people, remembered and forgotten, who have all had a part in shaping the people we have become.

The gift of failure may be a deep encounter with God. The biblical prophet Moses did not experience his theophany—his encounter with God made visible—when he was riding high as a prince of Egypt. His first encounter with God, his call, and his sending came when he had been brought low. He had fled Egypt as a murderer. Instead of winning the respect of his people, he had garnered their scorn and derision. He was no longer regarded as a prince. He was living in Midian as a fugitive and a hired hand when he saw the bush that was aflame but not consumed by fire.

It may be so for us also. It may be only when we have reached the end of our rope that we finally realize that the only secure handhold is God. When we recognize that we can no longer rely on our own resources, we open a space for God to work. When the myth of being self-made explodes in our face, we can fully awaken to the abiding presence of God. At times like these, failure is a blessing. When pride in our skill or good fortune has taken hold of us, failure may knock us to our knees and bring us to our senses.

But sometimes failure is not a blessing dressed as a curse. When love, faith, and work cannot hold two people together, a failed marriage is the devastating result. When lectures, blandishments, and punishments cannot curb a wayward child, the outcome may be a ruined life. When the best efforts of the defense team still end in a guilty verdict for an innocent person, the failure of the justice system can end in jail or even death. When dire illness does not yield to medical intervention, the failure of treatment ends a life. When people have done all that is humanly possible to achieve success and have fallen short, the gift is hard to discern. In fact, there may be no gift in failure for the people most directly affected.

And failure does not always surrender its gifts in the moment. The lessons of failure can be hard to learn. We may have to endure the same pain two, three, or more times for the teaching to take hold. The failure of the global community to halt the Nazi holocaust made world leaders say "never again." The failure to halt the Rwandan genocide prompted us to say "never again" again. We did not learn the lesson the first time. We may not yet have grasped the lesson of our failure fully. But now there is a global community that will not let the horror of Darfur be smothered in silence. Now there are world leaders who are not prepared to let tyranny reign unchecked in Burma/Myanmar. Now many voices raise the outcry about the fate of Tibet. Neither despots nor democrats can act with impunity. Even dictators cover themselves with the fig leaf of sham elections.

Each year we inch toward a more perfect way of living as a global community. Each year some places in the world succeed in the experiments in governance. Each year some countries fail miserably. Their leaders make no effort to uphold human rights. Their governments do not try to promote the well-being of the population. Despotic rulers are concerned with keeping the comforts of authority for themselves and their cronies. As long as people of conscience continue to call those in authority to account, the failure is miserable but not complete. For the failure of the human endeavor to be complete, it would have to be bound by the span of one human life. But we have already seen—in the lessons of holocaust, in cancer care, in the end of apartheid and the peace accord that ended the Troubles in Northern Ireland—that the Portuguese adage holds true: God writes straight on crooked lines.

No lines could be more crooked than those that tell the life of Jesus Christ. In human terms, Jesus's ministry was a failure. That failure is, in a sense, at the heart of Christian theology. The cross is a bloody and brutal failure. Jesus had shown such amazing love and compassion. He had really made a wonderful pitch for love. You would have thought that people would have seen what a tremendous guy he was. But that was not the result of his ministry. The end result, in human terms, was failure. It was a failure that seemed to be recognized even by the elements. The narratives that describe Jesus's death tell of a dark, lowering sky. Jesus, in a very human voice, cries out to God from the cross, "Why have you forsaken me?" Those are words that any one of us might have spoken from the depths of our disappointments. Jesus also speaks the words of faith "Into your hands I commend my spirit." He didn't know that there was going to be a resurrection. There was no hotline through which he heard the whisper "Don't fret, my son. It's going to be OK!" So he flung himself into what could well have been an abyss. His disciples had abandoned him. One betrayed him, another denied him three times, and the rest fled. It all seemed a colossal failure.

Then there was Easter. Christian churches celebrate Easter, the feast of the Resurrection of our Lord, with joy and pageantry. The first disciples probably faced the risen Christ with more mixed emotions. The accounts of Jesus's life and death all note that his disciples deserted him upon his arrest. Peter had been with Jesus since the beginning of his public ministry. He had vowed to stand by Jesus no matter what. Jesus predicted that before the cock crowed the dawn of a new day Peter would have denied him three times. It was so. The women, who were the most courageous of those who had followed Jesus, stood at a distance at his crucifixion. Those who had been his closest friends were marked by betrayal. At the moment of truth they failed in their promises. For them the fact of a resurrected Jesus cannot have been an unalloyed joy.

The grief of Jesus's death and the guilt of their desertion and denial were feelings they could have learned to live with in due course. Human life is marked with failures large and small. Those mistakes and misdeeds either teach life lessons or remain as unhealed wounds on the psyche. What the disciples did not expect was to have to have to face the one they had betrayed in the sure knowledge that he knew of their betrayal. They had failed miserably. They must have come with more than a little trepidation to their first encounters with the risen Christ.

Failure can do one of two things to us: it can be a stepping-stone to success, or it can open a door to despair. Judas, who betrayed Jesus into the hands of the authorities, was so ravaged by shame and guilt that he killed himself. Peter, who denied that he even knew Jesus—let alone that he was a close friend and disciple—responded differently. His failure demolished the pride and bluster that had been his chief characteristics. He realized that, on his own, he really didn't amount to much. His newfound humility opened the space for God to use him. He became as the Christ had named him: the Rock upon which the church was built.

Peter may have had a moment of uncertainty. His failure might have made him unsure whether to run toward or away from the risen Christ. When we fail we may want to hide from God. But God does not turn away from us. God doesn't reject us. Our failures may give God a better a chance to get our attention. We assume that God keeps a scorecard of our successes and failures. We think that God operates as we do, ready to record and reward our accomplishments but equally ready—if not more ready—to punish our deficits.

Mystics and people of prayer through the ages have assured us that they hear God differently. The writer of the biblical book of Isaiah hears God's assurance: "My thoughts are not your thoughts, nor are your ways my ways." The English mystic Dame Julian of Norwich surprises us by saying, "There is no blame in God." Julian sees in God pity for the woe our wrongs create for ourselves and others, but no blame.

We may feel shame for the deficits and disappointments that are of our own making. We may want to apportion blame when our failures are not our fault. But God's ways are not our ways. God holds all eternity in mind, and God knows all our flaws and our weaknesses. Sometimes we count failure when God has something else in mind.

I had known from an early age what I wanted to do. I wanted to be a doctor. I had felt a strong urge toward that profession. Though I succeeded in earning admission to medical school, I failed to raise enough money to be trained as a doctor. I turned, instead, to teaching. I enjoyed teaching. My temperament and training seemed to suit me to that vocation. When the government instituted the iniquitous Bantu Education system for black South Africans, I could not continue to teach. My conscience would not allow it. I started training for ordained ministry. I would have dearly loved to be a doctor; I hope I would have been a good one. I counted my inability to attend medical school a failure. I considered the end of my teaching career a failure too. Only in retrospect have I come to know that neither event was a failure. The end of each opportunity was an opening for me to take a different path.

The measure by which we judge success or failure is not God's yardstick. In fact, success and failure are often more a testament to our own arrogance. We think we know what our lives are meant to be. We believe we know how God must use us. We have the plan. When our plan doesn't work, we are devastated. As my wise friend Oprah Winfrey says, "We spend so much time staring despairingly at the door that has just closed that we don't notice that hope has opened a window."

What might our lives feel like if we didn't march through them with a scorecard, keeping a tally of our failures and successes? How would it be to stop pretending omniscience? Can you imagine being able to trust that the outcome of your efforts will be right, whatever the outcome? Even when it looks as though every effort is marked with failure?

The bishop who pastored me through the first stage of my call to ordained ministry could have counted his efforts a failure. He worked hard to bring an end to apartheid and ensure justice for all South Africans. He died in England in 1980. That was before I won the Nobel Peace Prize in 1984. It was before F. W. de Klerk was elected president of South Africa in 1989. It was ten years before Nelson Mandela was released from prison in 1990. When he died, Ambrose Reeves was a deportee who could not return to South Africa. He was a faithful laborer who did not live to harvest the fruits of his labor.

When Ambrose Reeves was expelled from South Africa in 1960 he had long been a thorn in the side of the South African government. He had arrived in South Africa in 1949 to serve as the Anglican bishop of Johannesburg. Three years later his confrontations with the apartheid government began.

The Anglican Church had a long history of providing a high-quality education to Africans. The government recognized that such an education was subversive to the aims of the apartheid state. One of the lynchpins of that system of racial oppression was the Bantu Education policy. The policy did not pretend to afford black South Africans an education comparable to that of their white compatriots. Its goal was to educate black people for subservience, for serfdom. Reeves denounced the policy as the "intellectual crippling of a nation" and declared, "Whatever the cost, we must make it plain to the government, the members of our Church, and all the African people that we disagree so profoundly with the policy . . . that we cannot be party to it in any shape or form."

The Diocese of Johannesburg refused to sell its schools to the government, as the law demanded. Instead the diocese shut down all its schools. It was a lonely stand against injustice. Johannesburg was the only diocese to refuse to cooperate with the act that established segregated schools. Other dioceses and denominations sold their property to the government and ceded control of their institutions.

In 1956 Reeves entered another battle. Early one December morning, 155 people of all races were arrested and charged with high treason, a capital offense in apartheid South Africa. On the day of their arrest Bishop Reeves agreed to chair their defense fund. With his group he found the money to retain some of South Africa's finest legal minds to represent the accused. The fund was also quickly able to secure bail for the defendants. The trial dragged on for five years. By the time the verdict was read, Bishop Reeves had been expelled from the country.

He was deported the year of the massacre at Sharpeville. In so many ways that incident marked a turning point for South Africa. On March 21, 1960, police opened fire on a crowd gathered at the Sharpeville police station to protest the iniquitous pass laws. Sixty-nine people were killed, and almost two hundred were wounded. The police claimed they had come under attack. They maintained that they had shot the protesters in self-defense. But the evidence showed that most of the injured were shot in the back as they tried to flee. In the ensuing days and weeks Bishop Reeves worked tirelessly to ensure that the truth about the massacre was known. When he went home to England on a long leave, he used the opportunity to describe what he had seen to the European media.

He returned to South Africa in September 1960. Two days later he was rounded up by security police and deported.

Nothing that Ambrose Reeves did was crowned with spectacular success. In the wake of the Sharpeville massacre the state clamped down on dissent. It outlawed black political organizations and arrested black political leaders. The victims of the police excesses of that day received no redress. The treason trial did end in acquittals for all the accused. But less than two years later the Rivonia trial began. The Rivonia trial was named for the suburb of Johannesburg where most of the accused were arrested. Driven underground by banning, the African National Congress had decided to take up arms. They had formed *uMkhonto we Sizwe* or MK (the spear of the nation). Those who stood in the dock for the Rivonia trial were virtually the entire leadership of the MK. Many of them had been accused in the first treason trial. The Rivonia trial ended in convictions and life sentences for Nelson Mandela, Govan Mbeki, and six of their co-accused.

School segregation and the Bantu Education Act were put in place in spite of the refusal of Bishop Reeves and his Johannesburg diocese to cooperate in their implementation.

Had Ambrose Reeves failed? Yes and no. He had not achieved the outcomes he had hoped for, the ends he had planned, and the goals for which he had worked. But the seeds his actions planted bore fruit many years later.

Bantu Education became the flash point for protests that engulfed South Africa and began the unraveling of oppressive state control. The people tried for treason in the 1950s became icons of the struggle to end apartheid. Though silenced by the prison walls, they inspired antiapartheid campaigners around the world. The massacre at Sharpeville and the international publicity that it garnered brought apartheid to the attention of the world community. The campaigns to isolate South Africa played an inestimable part in securing our freedom. They began in the months after Sharpeville in response to that mayhem.

In the span of his life Ambrose Reeves failed. But each of his failures laid another paving stone on the path to a free South Africa. He did not achieve the outcomes for which he worked in his time in South Africa, or even in his lifetime. The change for which he strove did not come in time for him to see it. But he worked for the good. What he achieved was good enough in the short term. And, ultimately, what he accomplished was good and right.

"It's amazing how much you can accomplish when it doesn't matter who gets the credit!" insists the adage. It's still more amazing how much we can accomplish when we can let go of the illusion of our own omniscience, let go of the accomplishment tally, and live a surrendered life.

You do not need to be a churchman to live a surrendered life. All of us can trust that choosing goodness will always, ultimately, result in creating rightness. And anyone can decide to choose goodness. Anyone can decide to set aside the tally list of successes and failures—and the stress and anxiety that accompany the task of keeping the list current. None of us can see eternity. None of us knows with perfect clarity what the end will be. But when we choose goodness we can be certain that, in the fullness of time, the end will be right.

What would you concede if it didn't matter who got the credit? What would no longer matter if you were not hostage to the accomplishment tally? How much peace could you claim by trusting that the choices that you made for goodness would ultimately turn out right? Just picture the freedom that comes with living a surrendered life. A surrendered life is not effortless. One who lives a surrendered life applies oneself with all due diligence. But one who lives a surrendered life can trust that no effort will be in vain. Though the good end may not come in the span of one human life—or even of one generation—the good will be the end.

Whether we surrender our lives or we march forward, head down, to the beat of our own drummer, God's love reaches out to us. Even though God reaches out to us, we often turn away from God. That is sin. In the next chapter we will explore why God allows us to follow our own paths. I will begin with a story from my life as a college chaplain.

But first let us turn into the stillness and listen to God speak with the voice of the heart:

Failure and shame shut your eyes
So you can't see me.
Anguish and pain shriek with your voice
And you can't hear me.

Guilt makes you turn aside
And you think I have walked away.
But through it all I am right here,
Right here where you wept lonely tears for me,
Right here where you thought you didn't want me to be.
I AM.

"Why have you forsaken me?"
I hear the cry through all eternity.
Child, I am here.
I know what you are doing.
I weep for you when you slide away from all that is right,
when you turn your back on all that is good.
I weep for you.
I see the that harm you do.
In my hand I hold your hand.
In my hand I hold the hurting hand of the one you are harming.
Right now,
In this moment,
I stand between the two of you and neither of you see me.
In one hand I hold the hand of my beloved child
My dear one who is blinded by suffering.
In my other hand I hold the hand of my beloved child
My dear one whose savagery and shame hide me from sight.
But I am here
Beside you both,
Between, within, and all around you both.
I AM.

8

WHY DOES GOD LET US SIN?

O God, break the teeth in their mouths;
Let them vanish like water that runs away;
like grass let them be trodden down and wither,
Let them be like the snail that dissolves into slime;
like the untimely birth that never sees the sun. . . .
The righteous will rejoice when they see vengeance done;
they will bathe their feet in the blood of the wicked. (Ps. 58)

My shoulders shook with bitter sobs. I was grieving, defeated, angry, devastated, undone. It was a Saturday morning. I was in the small chapel at the Federal Theological Seminary, FedSem. The seminary, where I taught, was next to the campus of the University of Fort Hare, where I served as a chaplain. The chapel was a small, intimate space built for the brothers of the Community of the Resurrection. I had come here to rail against the authorities and remonstrate with God.

It had all started with one of those student protests. I don't even remember what they were protesting, so much was wrong. The once-proud Fort Hare boasted such alumni as Nelson Mandela, Govan Mbeki, and late ANC president Oliver Tambo as well as luminaries from all over sub-Saharan Africa. The university was founded in 1916 as a Western-style institution for tertiary education for black Africans. Although it was a racially segregated university, the hallmark of Fort Hare was academic excellence. In 1959 it was taken over by the Nationalist Party government and was transformed into a "bush college." It became an ethnic institution governed by the central tenet of Bantu Education: Africans deserve only an inferior education; they are to be educated only for servitude. The government packed the school's administration with Afrikaners. Black staff endured discrimination and poor working conditions. Untried young white men who came to Fort Hare to polish their résumés replaced the once-stellar faculty. They came raw from university and could test their pedagogic theories on the black students. The students' wry response to this outrage was reflected in the graffiti on campus: "Has Fort Hare gone to the dogs; or have the dogs come to Fort Hare?"

Some excess of the administration had prompted a shift from harmless graffiti to a sit-in. The students had taken up a station outside the administration building and refused to move until their demands were met. The administration responded that they would not negotiate with a mob. The students, they said, must appoint a representative delegation. The students were no fools. They recognized that anyone selected for the delegation would be regarded as a ringleader and would be punished. Even knowing the possible consequences, a young law student, Barney Pityana, volunteered to serve as a spokesperson. The students would not hear of it.

On Friday, September 6, 1968, three hundred students were told they had been suspended and must disperse. That afternoon the police arrived in their trucks with their vicious dogs. They charged at the youngsters. The students held their ground. They didn't run away. They were so calm, so impressive. They stood up and sang *"Nkosi Sikelel' iAfrica,"* the hymn "God Bless Africa," which has become part of our national anthem. Then they were taken away, one by one, to collect their luggage, and they were expelled from the university.

I remember rushing into town with Dr. Gqubule, another of the chaplains, to buy bread; we hadn't the money for much else. We chased the departing trains to give the loaves to the students so they would have something to eat for the long ride home. Once again it seemed that evil had triumphed. And I was in the chapel weeping—no, wailing. I was railing against the callous lackeys of apartheid, and wailing loud enough to rouse the whole of heaven.

The particular situation I describe is unique to my life and South Africa's history. But that emotional combination of anger and anguish that poured out in my prayer is a

130 MADE FOR GOODNESS

common experience. It is the emotional territory inhabited by the parent of a child who was bullied at school. It is the internal landscape of a homeowner after the break-in. It is the place of every person who stands powerless in the face of an outrage or injustice. The words of my angry prayers are probably also familiar. Most people have situations or times when they can pray the most bloodcurdling psalms with feeling. Many of us have called down the god of wrath and vengeance with our prayers.

The Psalter is a wonderful resource for just this reason. We are reminded that our rage does have a place in our prayer life as it does in our emotional life. In their wisdom the compilers of the book of Psalms did not edit out the ugliest of sentiments. Instead, the bloody violence of one psalm is set next to the irenic lyricism of the next. The gift of the Psalter is that it permits us to pray our most murderous feelings and not act them out. The Psalter attests to the fullness of human experience. In the psalms we see what is so often our operational theology: the actions that show what we believe about God.

What the psalms show and our prayers indicate is that very often our operational theology describes a god who is less than God. Our operational theology describes a god of human making. Our prayers call forth a god who is on a human scale. We operate as though God is our lackey, available to demolish our enemies, fete our friends, and confirm our prejudices. We pray as if God were our wayward teenage child whose friends we must approve. We are not the first to behave in this manner. The psalms and so much of biblical literature describe a god who clobbers the writer's enemies, exacts punishment on unbelievers, and gives sinners their just deserts. It is a comfortable and comforting version of God.

This retributive God accords with our understanding of goodness. We understand goodness to be so opposed to evil and wrong that it cannot tolerate the existence of sin or sinners. This is true. Evil is repulsive to good. What we find harder to assimilate is that the good God is on the side of the sinner. But this is exactly what the Bible is telling us. God is on our side. God is not looking for reasons to punish us, as we deserve. God is, rather, looking for ways to redeem us from the prison of our errors. Instead of being the chief prosecutor, God is the lead defense attorney, if not the doting mother of the miscreant. God's love for sinners is hard for us to take in. It is hard because we have still not been able grasp the fact that God does not love us because we are good. God loves us because God loves us.

The reminder of God's unmerited and unconditional love struck me forcefully a short while ago. I was on retreat, and my spiritual director, Sister Maureen, had given me the fifteenth chapter of Luke's Gospel to read. It is the chapter that contains the story that we have spoken of earlier, the one about the prodigal son. I have read that parable many, many times over the years. I was amazed that I had not really seen the power of that introduction. The narrator tells us that the religious leaders were upset with Jesus because he welcomed sinners. He welcomed them! Can you see what that says about God? We are being told that God is not waiting to clobber us. In fact, just the opposite is true. God reaches out to us while we are wrapped in wrong! God takes the initiative. God does take the initiative in everything. In the relationship between God and humanity, God chose us. God chose us before we were there, before the foundation of the world. God said, "You are going to be mine." There is never a time when God says, "I will wait; I will hold back my affection until you are more deserving."

We often operate from the premise "I want to be good in order for God not to be mad at me, or so that God can approve of me." We really don't get it. God is, rather, yearning to embrace us. We reckon that somehow, somewhere, there's a catch. There must be a catch; it's too good to be true. It is unbelievable because in our lives it's not the kind of thing that happens. Our experience of other human beings, for instance, is that if they can get one over on you they will. And if they can drive you into a corner, embarrass you, and beat you, they won't need a second invitation. So we extrapolate and reckon that must be true of God.

On a recent trip to the Solomon Islands we visited the prison there. I told the prisoners, "God loves you. Do you know that you are the most precious thing in God's sight? God has no one more beautiful than you." When we left, one of our companions said that the prisoners had probably not heard anyone say that of them in long while, if ever. Yet it is true of them as it is true of each of us.

When we really grasp the truth of God's unconditional love, it can leave us breathless. It has left me breathless. It has amazed me. It has awed me. When we truly apprehend

God's love for the sinner—when we really get it—it almost doesn't make sense. The parable of the lost sheep underlines God's love for the sinner even more than the parable of the prodigal son. In the latter story God waits. God waits for the minutest sign of repentance. God waits for the smallest inkling that we are turning toward God. But the God of the prodigal parable does wait. As we have seen, the message in that story is God's reverence for human autonomy. The parable of the lost sheep is different. In that story God goes out after the lost sheep. There is no hint that the sheep plans to return. In fact, the lost sheep is intent on going away. The good shepherd leaves his ninety-nine perfectly well behaved sheep to set out in search of the lost one. God pursues the beloved who has gone astray. God leaves the saints to go in search of the sinner.

This love is what is so hard for us to fathom or to grasp. God's behavior, seeking out the sinner, undermines our notion of right and wrong. That the shepherd would abandon the obedient sheep to go and hunt for the recalcitrant one makes it seem to us that right and wrong do not matter. It seems that there is no benefit to doing right and there is no cost to doing wrong. But right and wrong do matter.

The benefit in doing right is the joy of pleasing the beloved. It is the thanksgiving we return for the love we have received. The price of doing wrong is paid both by the sinner and by God. For the sinner the price is alienation. Sin opens a chasm between the sinner and God. That distance is anathema to God. God does not see only our sin. God sees the good that has been covered up, distorted, blurred by our misdeeds. God knows that there is something in us that does not acquiesce in sin. Dame Julian calls it a "divine will" that resides in us. That divine will cannot and never will sin. So God sets out to close the gap that sin has opened between us. This pursuit of the wrongdoer is a costly pursuit. There is always the danger of loss. There is always the possibility that the ninety-nine will be lost while the shepherd chases after the one. There is always the possibility that the good will turn away while God seeks out the bad. There is always the possibility that the son will be killed to ransom the sinner. It is an extraordinary notion of goodness. God is willing to sacrifice the good to win the bad. God's love of the sinner is a costly, risky love.

God's pursuit of the sinner is a risky gamble, but it is not a futile one. God is no fool. God would not risk everything on a gamble that was doomed to fail. In fact, the early Christian theologian Origen would maintain that the odds are in God's favor. And time is on God's side. Origen believed that God's love is so irresistible that heaven will ultimately win us all. He scandalized his contemporaries by asserting that at the end of time even Satan would abandon hell to worship God in heaven.

Perhaps we, too, are shaken by the thought that our enemies will not burn in Hades throughout eternity. But, ultimately, the reality of heaven cannot tolerate the existence of hell. Even our worst enemies are God's beloved children. What kind of God could endure the sight of God's own children screaming in eternal pain? If we believe in the good

God, we must believe that we are all made to inhabit heaven. We are made for goodness.

We will not be driven into heaven by the fear of hell; rather, we will be drawn into heaven by the love of God. The power of evil will ultimately become unattractive, and we will yield to the beauty of heaven. So God's sacrifice is costly in time and it is worthwhile in eternity. It is risky in time, but the outcome is assured in eternity. At the end of time we must succumb to God. So God is willing to sacrifice everything to win us to the place where we are meant to be.

God calls to us throughout all ages. God woos us to goodness in the voices of prophets, apostles, martyrs, and evangelists. God coaxes us in the quiet voice of conscience.

"Did you have to scold so harshly?"

"Was that comment necessary?"

"Did you have to be so judgmental?"

"What does it cost you to smile?"

"Go ahead, say you are sorry. It won't hurt you."

"What does it cost to forgive?"

Azim Khamisa may have asked that last question. He buried his only son in accordance with his Muslim faith. On a rainy day in 1995 he climbed into the muddy pit holding Tariq's shrouded body. For a long time he stood cradling his burden, grieving his boy's lost life. "I did not want to climb out of that grave alone," he said. But he did. Tariq was gone.

In a California jail a teenage boy was awaiting trial. Fourteen-year-old Tony Hicks had shot and killed Tariq Khamisa. Tony didn't have a father who might grieve his demise. His mother was fifteen when Tony was born. His early years were scarred by violence and loss. A favorite cousin died in a hail of bullets when Tony was nine. He had watched the coroners carry his cousin's lifeless body away. When he was ten he moved across the country to live with his grandfather. The absence from his mother saddened and angered him. His grandfather's love and guidance were not enough. By the time he turned fourteen he had cast his lot with a gang of boys. Drink, drugs, and guns were, it seemed, essential ingredients of what they called fun. On January 21, 1995, twenty-one-year-old Tariq delivered a pizza to Tony's door. When Tariq refused to surrender the food without payment, the drunk, drugged teenager shot and killed him.

What does it cost to forgive? Ask Azim. He forgave Tony. Azim Khamisa established the Tariq Khamisa Foundation to honor his son. Now Azim Khamisa travels the country with Tony's grandfather, Ples Felix. They tell their story and speak about the power of forgiveness. They teach young people about the power of nonviolence.

Azim acts like the father Tony never had. He is working diligently to secure an early release of the person who killed his child. Azim's effort is as much as any father might pour into securing freedom for his only son, if Tony were his son.

Azim Khamisa gives us a glimpse of God's own conviction. In spite of the evil we do, there is a goodness in us that is unstained by sin. So the good shepherd will set off in search of the lost sheep. The father will run to meet the prodigal son though he is yet far off. In the next chapter we will see how, when we have strayed from goodness, we can find our way home. I will begin by sharing with you a story about my father and me.

But first let us turn into the stillness and listen to God speak with the voice of the heart:

Why are you running, running, running?
Why are you hiding away?
You may think that what you have done is beyond my power to
  forgive.
You may think what you have said makes me shrug and turn away.
You may think that you are lost.
But you are not lost to me.
How could you ever be?
Where are you that I cannot go?
Where have you been that I have not been?
What did you see that I have not seen?
What did you do?
No, it cannot be undone,
The pain cannot be unmade,
The life cannot be un-lived,
The time will not run backward,
You cannot un-choose your choice.
But the pain can be healed,
Your choices can be redeemed,
Your life can be blessed,
And love can bring you home.

9

GOING HOME
TO GOODNESS

We were at the wrong end of a very long day. I was in
no mood for a serious conversation with my father.
We were returning from Swaziland. I just wanted to drive
the remaining few kilometers to my mother-in-law's home
and go to bed. The trek from Alice to Swaziland and back
had become a quarterly ritual for our family. After a blissful
sojourn in England, where the children had enjoyed integrated schools, we had returned to South Africa and Bantu
Education. Neither Leah nor I could countenance subjecting
our children to that inferior pap, so we sent the three oldest
children to boarding schools in neighboring Swaziland.

The drive from Alice to Swaziland was grueling. We left
Alice at 4 a.m. to avoid being in the Karoo, that vast arid ex-

panse, in the heat of the day. No South African hotels would accommodate a black family. We had to drive almost fifteen hours from Alice to my parents' home near Johannesburg. We would spend the night there and then drive the ten-hour round trip to the children's schools in Swaziland the following day. We would overnight in Johannesburg before setting off, once again, for home.

We were at the end of the third leg of that journey, having made the round-trip to Swaziland that day. Those were the days before mobile telephones. Telephones were very few and far between in the black townships and neither my parents nor any of their near neighbors had a telephone. The stop at my parents' home was a courtesy call to allay their worries about our cross-border journey.

"I'm tired and I have a headache coming on. Please can we talk tomorrow?" I bundled Leah and Mpho into the car and we drove off to spend the night with my mother-in-law in Kagiso several kilometers away.

The next morning my sister's daughter, Sylvia, roused us before dawn. She lived with my parents and had been sent from Munsieville to bring the news. My father, Mkhulu, was dead.

I was doubly devastated by the loss. In spite of all the hurts and complications of our relationship, I loved my father. I delighted in his stories, and I admired his wisdom. He was clever, and loving, and witty. There was so much about him that I would miss. I had failed my father. I could have sat and talked to him. Whatever he had to say, would it have taken more than a few minutes? More than an hour?

What did he need to say? I had made him leave this life carrying his concern with him. He had died leaving those words unspoken. And I had lost the opportunity to ever talk to my father again. I wanted to kick myself!

I know that we don't always have time for the ones we love. We rush to end a telephone conversation with a spouse because a meeting looms. We cut short story time with the children to finish up a report for work. We skip the opportunity to play or be with friends because we are tired. That's not sinful, it's sanity. But this time it mattered. It stung. This was Thokoza and the old woman's death all over again. Would I never learn?

All these years later Mpho asked if I've forgiven myself. I had to answer that I don't know. I know that God has forgiven me. But I am betwixt and between. If I forgave myself, would it mean that I had taken my transgression too lightly? Would it show that I hadn't understood the gravity of my fault? I almost feel annoyed with God. "How can God forgive me? God just doesn't understand. These things are serious!"

"I know better than God!" says my unforgiving, arrogant heart. When I hear my thoughts, I recognize disapproving voices of the religious leaders and teachers of Jesus's own community. Like the critics and carpers described in the introduction to the story of the prodigal, I am surprised and annoyed that Jesus is welcoming a sinner. I am especially surprised because that sinner is me.

In the Christian lexicon, sin is that which separates us from God. To sin is, in a sense, to run away from home.

Goodness is our home. Like the godly perfection we described in an earlier chapter, the goodness that is our true heart and home bears only a fleeting resemblance to the "being good" of our guilty musings. I am supposedly "being good" when I skip the rum-raisin ice cream I want in favor of the salad I detest. (I am no fan of rabbit food. Blagh!). There is a certain pursed-lipped superiority to this flavor of "goodness." It leeches every ounce of joy from life.

The goodness that is our true home has no finger wagging attached to it, and no reproachful "should." The striving and shame that are hallmarks of "being good" are replaced by wholeness and the experience of being at peace with ourselves, at home in our own skin. Even now, thinking about the night my father died makes me want to crawl out of my skin. My father was, by then, an old man. *Ubuntu* and half a thought would have stayed my step. My father had humbled himself to ask for a hearing. He had reached out to me. How much would it really have cost me to sit awhile? How much might our relationship have gained?

Conflict with parents is an almost inevitable part of human life. When we are young their guidance may seem like arbitrary constraint. When we become teenagers their strictures collide with our desire for freedom. As we grow to adulthood they may not agree with our life choices. We may not agree with theirs. Over the years there are so many opportunities for irritations to flare and for hurts to go unhealed. But when we are in conflict with our parents, the very fabric of our lives is woven amiss. When we are able to accept our parents, when we can regard them with compassion, we can begin to be more fully in harmony with our world.

The Buddhist teacher Thich Nhat Hanh offers the following meditation, a gift to those who have unhealed or unforgiven fights with parents dead or alive. He invites you to imagine your parent as a five-year-old child. Imagine this child as fully as you are able. Bring all you know of your parent's early life to this meditation. Bring a sense of his joys, his fears, and his sadness. See your parent as a five-year-old child, and regard this child with compassion. Know that hidden in the person your parent has become is that five-year-old child. Hidden inside the adult is the child with all her happiness, all her worries, and all her unhealed hurts. As you allow your heart to open and soften toward that child, your heart can begin to soften toward your parent. You can turn to face him or his memory with compassion. As we are able to see our parents' goodness and forgive them for their failings, we are better able to see our own goodness and forgive ourselves for our failings.

Finding our way back to ease inside ourselves, finding our way home to goodness, will be a journey we will have to make often. Every day, in small slips and large lapses, we part from what we know is good. The things that draw us away from our best selves are habits. We slide into habits of thought. We fall prey to patterns of behavior. The errors that we make once we are apt to repeat. It is not novelty that tempts us. We are so predictable in our vices. We constantly stumble over the same stone. Pride tells us that we know how to navigate around our faults. But time and again we find ourselves falling over the same failing. And then, like the prodigal among the pigs, we come to our senses. We recognize what we have done and consider who we have become. Then we can decide to make the journey home.

T'shuva ("returning") is the Hebrew word in the Bible that describes finding our way back to goodness. We return to ourselves, to our godliness, to wholeness. We may set out on our way back convinced that the journey will take a lifetime. We recognize that we have wandered so far from home, from good, from God. We have so much to do to become the people God intended us to be. Recognition is the first step of the journey home. The second step is reorientation. The return to goodness requires that we turn around.

Christian theologians use the word *repentance* or the Greek word *metanoia* to describe this act of reorientation. *Metanoia*, or repentance, literally means "rethinking." Many things might prompt us to rethink our words or actions. Perhaps the response to our words or tone prods our remorse. As a parent, Mpho has experienced those times when the children seem determined to "drive her over the edge." Of course, *I know* my grandchildren can do no wrong, but I humor her with sympathetic murmurs.

It does not seem so long ago that her mother and I were the ones challenged to keep our cool while Mpho tried to drive us over the edge. I remember one occasion when Mpho was young and her chattiness had strained us to breaking point. "Do shut up, Mpho. You talk too much," I snapped irritably. Undaunted, the four-year-old whipped back, *"You* talk too much, Daddy. You stand up and talk all by yourself in church." Her unwitting wittiness surprised us into laughter.

Of course, our children are not always quite so clever, and we have the task of dragging ourselves back from the edge. We must stifle the angry word while it is still in our mouths. This does not mean we must resist discipline. But we must ask ourselves: Is my intent truly loving discipline—consistent with the parental duty to instruct? Or do I just want to punish the child? Do I want to inflict pain and suffering and exact retribution?

Sometimes when restraint fails we whip out a biting reprimand. Then we see the child wither in the face of our rage. Though what we said may have been true of our target, the way we said it wasn't true of us. So we rethink what we have said or how we have said it. We turn away from what we have done and face in a different direction. We reorient ourselves. It is so easy. But it is so hard.

Reorientation and returning are hard both for the person who inflicts harm and for the person harmed. Returning to goodness, recovering wholeness are tasks for both of them. When I cause a hurt, it is hard for me to stop, repent, and return. I must gather up the shards of damaged or broken relationship that injury implies and begin the work of restoration. When I have been harmed, I also need to gather myself up from brokenness. Whether I inflict the harm or I am the one who is hurting, I need to be restored to wholeness.

Perpetrator and victim are not always fixed labels. In the heat of argument Leah and I can each say some hurtful things to the other. Who is injured? Who is at fault? Both of us are. Each of us has hurt. Each of us is hurt. Each of us and both of us together need to gather ourselves up from brokenness and be restored to wholeness. We both need to find our way back to goodness.

When a person endures an extreme or traumatic injury, the brokenness can be expressed as dissociation. Psychiatrists recognize dissociation as a mental malady. Pastors know it as a spiritual dearth. One woman testified to the Truth and Reconciliation Commission that, after experiencing days of horrific torture at the hands of the South African security police, she "was like a person who was physically there but spiritually and mentally wasn't there."

Another, named Zola, said, "They tortured my body but it wasn't me. I left Zola safe in a corner of the cell. I didn't take her when I got out of prison. I came to the Truth Commission to get Zola back. I came to reclaim myself." For both these women something shattered in the trauma, something that needed to be gathered up, collected, healed.

Few of us have experienced trauma this great. But all of us dissociate in some way when we forget or abandon our innate goodness. In doing so we step away from wholeness. An essential part of us is silenced, denied, or ignored. While the quantum of anguish may change, the characteristics stay the same. Whether we endure torture or we face a workplace dispute, we experience harm and suffering. It is not the fact of the feelings that differs; it is the degree. Our relationships and we must be healed through the same process of admitting the wrong, witnessing the misery, asking for forgiveness, and restoring the relationship.

I look back on more than fifty years of marriage and see my own growth and evolution. It is not that I do no wrong (much as I would like to think that is true). Nor has it become easier to admit when I am wrong. It hasn't even become easier to ask for forgiveness. But over the years, as we have nurtured our love and I have cultivated my own conscience, I find that I do not stew over slights and hurts for hours or days. The instant of recognition comes sooner. The journey to apology and restoration is shorter than it once was. This can be true for anybody. Anyone can make the decision to be more mindful of his words and deeds and of their effects. Anyone can choose to cultivate compassion. Anyone can commit herself to returning ever more speedily to the goodness that is her true home.

In an extraordinary way, we can return to goodness more quickly when we have a clear vision of the present. That clarity about the present is rooted in making peace with the past. Putting words to our pain begins the process of building that peace. In speaking the truth of our pain, we start to collect the memories of what we have done or experienced. When we retell our stories we can be heard into healing. We can be heard back to wholeness, back to goodness, back home to ourselves.

Being heard into healing was the experience of many victims of torture or their surviving family members at the Truth and Reconciliation Commission hearings. For the victims to tell the story of what they had endured was an opportunity for healing, an opportunity to recover the dignity lost in the terror of torture. For some of the surviving family members of those who had been killed, the hearings provided closure. For many of them it was the first time they heard how their beloved had died and why.

Surprisingly, many of the perpetrators began their own healing journeys at the witness table. They spoke there of deeds that they had allowed to come to mind only in nightmares: "I really had bad dreams. I have dreams of bodies or parts of bodies, like an arm. This is a recurring dream. I still have it now. An arm sticking out of the ground and I'm trying to cover it up and there were people around and I know that I killed them. Whatever is down there and it's been down there for weeks and it is this intense feeling of guilt and horror that this thing has come out of the ground again, and I had a dream that I actually met a guy that I shot." For South African Counter-Insurgency officer John Deegan, speaking of the horrors that he had committed was like waking from the nightmare: "It's enough now!" It was the first step on his healing journey.

Being heard into healing is a need experienced not only by the perpetrators of heinous crimes. It is a basic human need that we all share. If we are lucky or blessed, we find people with the gift of presence. These are people who can hear us into healing. My wife, Leah, has the gift of presence. The kitchen tables in our various homes have been the sites of many confessions. Women of every sort have come to sit with Leah to share their joys and tell their woes. Her offer of a cup of tea and her willingness to hear without feeling compelled to judge or advise begins their healing journeys. All the agonies of life are poured out to her. Those roiling in the pain of marital infidelity, the parental agony that meets the angst of a teenage child, the effects of arguments at work and fights at the dinner table all find their way to Leah's gracious presence. Somehow, in the warmth of her hug or the calm of her still dignity, the healing begins.

Leah has the gift of presence, but we can all cultivate the qualities that constitute the art of hearing into healing. We can decide to hear with compassion and without judgment. We can recognize that sometimes it doesn't matter what we think. Sometimes things are not right or wrong; they just are.

Often people come to us not asking for advice or counsel. We don't have to have the answer. We don't have to solve the problem. They just want a listening ear. A listening ear can help people to work out their own wisdom. A friend who serves as a chaplain is surprised by the number of times she emerges from a hospital room with the patient's words of gratitude ringing in her ears: "You were so helpful." "I didn't do anything," she confides, "I just sat, listened, and smiled, or sighed, and nodded. They figured it all out for themselves."

Sometimes it is in sharing how we are affected by her story that we open the door for another person's healing. Our tears when someone tells us his pain may assure him that he is not crazy. "Yes," our tears say, "your feelings are valid." Sharing our own experiences can offer the comfort of knowing that she is not alone.

"When I have argued with my wife . . ." Mpho says she was surprised by the retreat leader's idle comment. It was a revelation. She knew this person, knew his rock-solid marriage. Intellectually, she knew that he almost certainly argued with his wife. Mpho says she found that those words were a comfort as she navigated a period of marital tension. "Of course married people argue." It was just comforting to know that those particular married people, married people with names and faces, argued. Moments that offer us glimpses into other people's personal struggles underline our shared humanity and open the door to welcome us home.

The journey homeward to healing can traverse some rough terrain. When the wounds are large or deep, a salve is necessary to speed us along the road to health. Forgiveness can be the richest kind of healing balm. We miseducate ourselves and our children with the trite phrase "Forgive and forget." Forgiveness is not a form of forgetting. It is, rather, a profound form of remembering. When we forgive, we remember who and whose we are. We remember that we are creative beings modeled on a creative God.

When we forgive, we reclaim the power to create. We can create a new relationship with the person who has injured us. We can create a new story of ourselves. When we find the strength to forgive, we are no longer victims. We are survivors.

Forgiveness is not only a creative act; it is a liberating action. When we forgive the people who have harmed us, we liberate ourselves from the chains that bind us to our offender. We don't hold their offenses against them. And they exert no control over our moods, our disposition, or us. They have no further part in writing the story that we must tell of ourselves. Forgiveness liberates us. We are free.

The same can be said of forgiving ourselves. We may learn from the practice of forgiving others how to forgive ourselves. Or we may extend the same forgiveness we offer ourselves to other people. It does not matter where we first set foot on this circle of compassion. The better we are able to forgive ourselves for our faults and failings, the better we are able to forgive others. The more we forgive others for their sins and shortcomings, the more we learn to forgive ourselves.

The hard tangle of emotions that I bring to the memory of my father's acts of violence stretches its tentacles over my inability to fully forgive myself for not letting him speak to me that last night. The more my heart softens toward one, the more it softens toward the other. Compassion combs the knots of pain out of my memories. Increasingly I face the man I was and the father I had with forgiveness. In time we will both be free.

When we forgive, we claim the power to create: we create a new relationship. When we forgive, we claim the power to liberate: the people who have harmed us are no longer beholden to us, and we are no longer bound to them. When we forgive, we reclaim memory: we remember that we are good; we remember how to be whole. We also literally re-member our family, our community, and ourselves. Family squabbles can have us casting our spouses or siblings into the outer darkness. Hurt or anger can make a parent disown her child or a child disown his sibling. Forgiveness allows them to re-member each other; to reclaim their place as members of one family.

The story of the prodigal son illustrates how, with a choice of words, we can deny common membership in a family unit. Though his father rejoiced at his return, the older brother of the prodigal was not so free with his welcome.

He confronts his father: "For all these years I have worked hard and toed the line. Have you ever done a thing for me? But now this wanton son of *yours* comes back and you throw him a party!" he says. His words "this son of *yours*" highlight the relationship between father and child and subtly disavow the sibling relationship. But the father re-members his sons, draws them back into common membership of one family. "My son, we had to celebrate. This brother of yours was dead and now he is alive. He was lost and has been found!"

The Truth and Reconciliation Commission witnessed some incredible acts of re-membering. One such act was a generous gift from the mother of a slain boy. In 1986 seven boys were massacred in a police ambush in Gugulethu Township outside Cape Town. In the weeks before that ambush the boys had been befriended by an *askari*, a captured activist who had been coerced into police service. The *askari* had encouraged them to raid the local police headquarters. After ten years of repeated denials, two police officers came to the TRC to admit their roles in the premeditated slaughter. After the hearings one of the policemen, Thapelo Mbelo, asked to meet with the mothers of the slain boys. "*Ndi cel'uxolo,*" he said. "I ask forgiveness." Literally, "I ask for peace." The Xhosa locution recognizes that forgiveness not only establishes peace between the offender and the injured party; it also creates the possibility of peace in the offender's psyche. One of the mothers began her response *"Mtan'am,"* "My child." With that simple phrase she re-membered him. She drew Thapelo back into the community from which his own cruelty had excluded him.

Forgiveness and re-membering open the door to the ambitious ongoing work of reconciliation. The word itself, *re-conciliation*, indicates a restoration. It implies the restoration of cordial relations that existed before the breach. But in many places what existed before was not comity or concili-ation. What existed before was something else that was less than ideal. For the writers of the biblical creation stories, human history offered no examples of true conciliation. Their knowledge reached back across a landscape sodden with the blood of war and the torment of slavery. So they looked back instead to a time before time. They imagined the ideal, the time when all creation lived in harmony with God in the Garden of Eden. When we reconcile, we inhabit that territory conceived by the hope-filled imagination. We meet again as for the first time. Eden is not an unattainable ideal. It is a place that most of us have seen, even if only fleetingly.

The delicious days when love is new are like Eden in their freshness. We can experience the wonder of Eden at the birth of a child or when a nature-scape takes our breath away. We can know the harmony of Eden when we gather with friends and family for times of celebration. For our family weddings, birthdays, and anniversaries offer a glimpse of Eden. Recently friends from many periods of our life together gathered to help Leah and me celebrate fifty years of marriage. The Soweto church was filled with people of every age, every color, from every continent and many faiths. We had, in that place, a view of primeval harmony.

For one of Mpho's seminary professors, Eden, the time before time, occurred in the delight-filled days of his courtship. He and his fiancée visited a marriage therapist: "We want you to see and remember who we are when we are happy. If, in the course of our marriage, we should lose our joy, you will know what we have lost. You will know how to help us find it again."

Even in South Africa, where the "before" of our experience was apartheid, a reality we have no desire to reinhabit, we had glimpses of Eden. Disparate organizations worked together with common purpose. People of faith from across the religious spectrum set aside their differences to oppose the evil machinations of the government. Many, many individuals defied unjust laws to uphold family life, human dignity, health, and well-being. Still, our task in the new South Africa is to build the "before" of our imagination, an Eden where all that is created can flourish. Eden has not taken root in South Africa, so the work begun in our Truth and Reconciliation Commission has not yet ended.

Indeed, reconciliation is the work that does not end. Linda Biehl described the unglamorous dailiness of that work to Mpho. Linda's daughter, Amy, was killed in South Africa. Blond, slim, and pretty, Amy Biehl was the stereotypical vision of a California girl. It was her passion for justice, her academic ability, and a Fulbright scholarship that took her to South Africa. She worked on voter education and registration in advance of our first nonracial election. The day before she was due to board a plane for California, Amy drove some friends home to Gugulethu, the black township outside Cape Town where the seven boys were murdered. Neither Amy nor her friends knew about the protest march that was taking place that day. "One settler, one bullet!" chanted the angry mob. A hail of rocks and stones halted Amy's car. She was dragged from the car, beaten, and stabbed. She died in a police station a continent away from her California home.

Four young men were convicted of her murder. They admitted to having inflicted the stabs that killed her. The new South Africa has no death penalty. They were sentenced to prison. When the Truth and Reconciliation Commission was formed, the young men applied for amnesty (on the grounds that theirs was a political act). Linda and Peter Biehl, Amy's parents, traveled to South Africa to support the amnesty application. The appeal was granted.

To honor Amy's life and her commitment to the vision of a Rainbow Nation, where people of every race could live together with dignity, the Biehls established the Amy Biehl Foundation. It has operations in the United States and in the South African township where Amy was killed. Amy's father, Peter, died in 2005. Linda now spends much of her year in South Africa. Two of Amy's killers work with Linda at the foundation in Cape Town.

For Linda Biehl, reconciliation is not an abstraction. Every day of the year she wakes up and her child is dead; on many days she knows that she is going to get up and be with the people who killed her daughter; and on some days, she says, she has to forgive them all over again. It's not a one-off thing. She didn't decide one day and in that instant complete the work of forgiveness and reconciliation. She told Mpho that it really is ongoing work. Forgiveness is work that Linda engages in every day as the mother of a slain child. Reconciliation is work that Linda has taken on as the head of her foundation. Her efforts draw us closer to that reconciled South Africa, that Eden where all our children can learn and laugh, love and live in the goodness that is God's gift to each of us and God's dream for all of us.

Finding our way back to goodness is ongoing work. To find our way home we will need a skilled guide. In the next chapter we will talk about how we have learned to hear God's guidance. I will begin by telling you about something important that happened to me when I was a teenager.

But first let us turn into the stillness and listen to God speak with the voice of the heart:

How far are you from Eden?
Which is the road home?
Come, child, I will show you.
See there, the path of humility,
The road of sorrows spoken,
The way of "sorry" said?

That way leads to Eden.
Do you see the path of pride?
The road trodden flat, marked out by
The ones who cannot be contrite,
The stiff-necked road of harsh, loud voice?
It passes far from Eden
With a mountain between to shelter it from sight.
How far are you from Eden?
Child, you will know.
When you have worn out the way of remorse
And retraced the path of repentance,
When you have pointed out the road for home
And pulled others onto the path,
Then you will know
Eden is not far from you.

10

HEARING
GOD'S VOICE

I knew where this story ended. I had seen the stretchers wheeled out of our general ward, sheets draped over lifeless faces. Cold bodies in the cold mortuary. I was sixteen or seventeen years old then, and I had been in this place for months. It was the men's ward at the Rietfontein tuberculosis hospital. I was in the bathroom coughing up blood. It was not just coming in isolated drops. I was hemorrhaging. The blood was coming like a flow. I knew what this signaled. The doctors knew it, too. "Your young friend is not going to make it," they had told Trevor Huddleston. They didn't have to tell me. I had seen it before. I knew. In the short shuddering breaths between coughs I spoke to God: "Well, God, if I'm going to die it's OK. And if not, that's OK too." I was surprised by the calm that flowed over me after I had spoken that prayer. I didn't feel brave. I just didn't feel desperate or anxious anymore. I wasn't clinging to life. I hadn't given myself up to death. I had just allowed myself to rest in God's presence, and I was at peace.

As the years have passed, my prayer seems to have come full circle. Most of the time, in prayer, I find that I am holding the world and my concerns before God. I do not offer God prescriptions—"Do this. Fix that"—though most of us would say there is much for God to fix and do. I know that. I read the daily papers, and I watch the news. I see all the pain and turmoil in the world. In one week there is flooding in one corner of our planet and drought-induced famine in another. Earthquakes and tidal waves are quickly pushed off the headlines by other natural disasters. Wars follow wars in a seemingly endless cavalcade. Rape, murder, hijacking, and mayhem of every sort are part of my daily news diet. I have children and grandchildren, travels, meetings, and presentations, all of these bring their own delights, cares, and concerns. Often I know what I want to have happen. Yet when I enter into my private time of prayer, I sit and offer all those plans, hopes, joys, and cares to God—not prescribing to God what should happen, but holding people and situations before God. I allow myself to become quiet. I just try to be.

Just "being," not "doing," is a real challenge to most of us. We have such busy, active lives. We pride ourselves on the length of our "to do" lists. We cram noise and activity into every waking minute. Even when our mouths are silent, our minds are busy with their own incessant chatter. Inside our heads we supply a running commentary on everything we see, feel, think, and experience. Prayer puts us in a receptive mode. As we still ourselves and let our yammering thoughts recede into the background, we can begin to hear the voice of God that has been speaking softly beneath the din of our demands.

The psalmist speaks in the voice of God: "Be still and know that I am God." That directive may be much easier offered than followed. When we try to still ourselves, our mind becomes a kitten skittering after each thought as though it were a mouse or a dangling piece of yarn. We are quiet for a moment; then a thought appears and our mind races off in pursuit, fascinated by the sparkle of our own wit. The mind needs to be guided away from distraction.

In the same way that we ready our children for sleep by using rituals that shut down the distractions of the day, small rituals can prepare our minds for prayer. Choosing and using a prayer place can be one such ritual. At home, in Soweto, I have a chapel, a place set aside for prayer. In Cape Town I have an oratory, a small nook that is my private prayer place. But I travel a lot, and so the ideal settings are not always available. I carry a cross and an icon—an image that is my companion in prayer. These physical things help to mark out a prayer place for me. My Muslim friends carry a prayer mat and create for themselves a sacred space in any place. You may not have a chapel or an oratory. Ideally, you want a private room. Even that may not always be available.

When you don't have a private room, the second ritual step, selecting a time, becomes all the more important.

Choose a time when you are unlikely to be interrupted. If possible, enlist help to make sure that you will be left alone. At home I wake before most of the household begins its day. While Leah sleeps beside me, I sit up in our bed and have some quiet time with God. When the children were young, Leah helped to guard my prayer times by keeping the children engaged in something that didn't involve me. She still constructs the rhythm of our home around my prayer times. My staff also constructs my meeting schedule around the times I set aside for quiet.

Once time and place have been set, the prayer can begin. When I sit down to pray, I usually begin my time with some form of invitatory—a prayer of invitation. One of my favorites is the Veni Creator Spiritus, or "Come, Creator Spirit":

Come, Holy Spirit, Creator blest,
and in our souls take up Thy rest;
come with Thy grace and heavenly aid
to fill the hearts which Thou hast made.

This and other prayers of invitation make explicit what is implied in prayer. We can pray only by the grace of God. We must enlist God's help to engage in conversation with God. Once I have made this invitation, I am ready to enter the stillness.

There are many ways to still oneself. Mpho teaches the use of breath and of the line of the Psalter that I mentioned earlier as a path into stillness. "Be still and know" is mouthed on a slow inhalation; "that I am God" is mouthed on the exhalation. The words are not spoken aloud. But mouthing the words helps to hold the attention. Although the words fall away, the inhalation and exhalation do not become shorter. Rather, breath fills the wordless space.

> *Be still and know that I am God*
> *Be still and know that I am*
> *Be still and know that I*
> *Be still and know that*
> *Be still and know*
> *Be still and*
> *Be still*
> *Be*

When Mpho uses this form of prayer, she will reconstruct the line word by word and then allow each word to fall away again in turn. Sometimes that construction and deconstruction will fill the whole period she has set aside for meditation. Sometimes the words fall away as she sinks into silence. On occasion the words fall away and then return as some distraction threatens to intrude on the stillness. The words and breath are like a banister in an uneven stairwell: sometimes one must lean on the banister heavily; other times a light touch is all that is necessary to steady one's step; still other times the railing is not needed at all. It is so with the words of the psalm and the attention to the breath: sometimes they are needed to push the chatter aside; sometimes they are a barely perceptible presence; sometimes they fall away completely. This kind of rhythmic repetition of a word, verse, or mantra is a prayer practice that anyone can use. When the repetition is paired with attention to the breath, it offers a path into deep silence. As we find and inhabit that silence, we will become more attuned to the voice of God.

I say that we will become attuned to the voice of God because it is a voice that is constantly present with us. God is talking to us all the time, always inviting us into conversation. We are a little like football fans at a game. The roar of the crowd is so loud it drowns out the comments of the person sitting right beside us. We must turn and give our seatmate our full attention in order to understand what she is saying. Prayer, then, is like turning to give our seatmate our full attention. When we enter into contemplative prayer, the crowd doesn't go away. The concerns and worries that we bring into our prayer time don't miraculously vanish. But the noise of them recedes. We have turned our attention to something more important. God's voice moves into the foreground.

My son-in-law—Mpho's husband, Joe—used to be a sportswriter for a national newspaper. For a long time he covered college basketball. He attended hundreds of games around the country. His favorite time of year was "March madness," when the teams played their championship tournament. It was a tense and exciting time of year. "I was almost always writing on deadline," he told me. When we watched a televised game together he pointed out the area where he usually sat: press row, right at the edge of the basketball court. I couldn't imagine how he did his job. The games were exciting. The players raced up and down the court, feet pounding, ball slamming the floor with loud thunks. They called to their teammates and shouted at their opponents. Coaches yelled instructions. Referee whistles shrilled. The fans screamed. The cheerleaders jumped about in incredibly boisterous and acrobatic displays. Sometimes balls, or players, would come crashing into the press table. "I had to write with all of that going on. I couldn't start writing when the game ended. That was when my story was due," Joe explained. "I treated it as background music. When I was writing on deadline I couldn't let the noise distract me. I had to follow the game, the plays. All the other stuff was just background music." Joe was able to create stillness in the midst of chaos. We do the same when we pray. The practice of prayer trains our hearts to hear and our eyes to see the pattern of God's speech. The practice of prayer draws the thread of goodness into the foreground and allows the clamor of our dreads and desires to become "background music."

Describing what we do as "the practice of prayer" serves as a reminder that none of us is expert at this. To the anxious question that Mpho and I are so frequently asked about prayer—"Am I doing it right?"—we can honestly answer, "Probably not. But it doesn't matter." The early Christian epistle writer Paul says in his letter to the Romans, "We do not know how to pray as we ought," but he goes on to assure his readers that "the Spirit helps us in our weakness . . . and intercedes with sighs too deep for words." So even though we are probably not doing it "right" when we pray, we are doing it well enough.

One of the ways of praying "well enough" is to turn our attention to God from time to time throughout the day. Small prayers remind us of our blessings. They halt us in our head-long rush through the day. They let us stop and savor little moments. Mpho's husband, Joe, wakes their daughters with the prayer "Thank you, God, for allowing us to see another day. Please take us through this day and keep us safe." Before meals our family is accustomed to offering a thanksgiving for the food and those who prepared it, and to pray for those in need. The first drive of the day is occasion for a travel prayer: "God bless us and all those who travel by land, or air, or water today, that our journeys may be safe. May we be a source of blessing for those we meet; may they be a source of bless-ing to us. In Jesus's name. Amen." Mpho and I have "pocket prayers." These are little prayers that carry us through the day. These are ways we are accustomed to address God.

Our days are full of transition times. We move from sleep to waking, from waking to washing, from washing to dressing, and on into the day. Many young children find these transitions difficult. Most parents and teachers will tell you that transitions are the most stressful times of the day for children. Those are the times when tantrums and meltdowns are most apt to happen. As we get older, either we learn to manage the transitions or we learn to mask or transfer our stress.

You may have noticed in the prayers I have described that our practice is to pray our transitions: we mark our movement from one thing to the next with a prayer. Both Mpho and I pray in the morning when we rise. We offer a prayer of thanksgiving before meals. We have a prayer before we begin the first journey of the day. We begin meetings with a prayer. If necessary, if we need to reorient our deliberations, we interrupt meetings to pray. We offer prayers in the evening and before we go to sleep. If your family or corporate culture will not welcome the opportunity to pray, a minute of silence may be very welcome. My friends at the Fetzer Institute—a foundation that works to foster awareness of the power of love and forgiveness in the world—begin all their meetings with a time of silence. Mpho calls it "a time to arrive." In the silence, the people who are gathered can mentally set aside the concerns and issues that are not germane to the task at hand. They can become fully present for the meeting. The silence prepares the gathering for fuller communication.

Prayer is how we communicate with God, and how God communicates with us. Communication is a skill. It must be cultivated and practiced. After more than half a century of happy marriage I can say, without fear of contradiction, that I am still learning how to communicate with my wife. In our life together there is so much that goes unspoken, so much that is open to interpretation—and misinterpretation. In the course of any day there is so much that she says, in words or wordlessly, that I miss or misunderstand. As the years have progressed, our mutual understanding has been deepened by love and shared history. There are conversations we no longer need to have. There are things we can take as given.

But I am no longer as young as I was once. The years have dulled my hearing and dimmed my vision. I do not see as well as I once did, and despite the ministrations of some wonderful doctors, my hearing is no longer as acute as it was in my youth. It used to be that a facial expression or a whispered cue was enough for Leah to convey a piece of vital information to me. Now the facial expression is accompanied by a touch, and the whisper is underlined with a subtle nudge. We are learning new ways to communicate.

It is so with God, who speaks to us now in one way now in another. It is so with us. We address God in the quiet of our hearts, in hymns and psalms, in dance and chant, with tears, with pleas, and with rejoicing. Each day as I return to the practice of prayer I learn new ways to hear God. Each day I learn new ways to address God.

———————

You will know from earlier chapters that the quiet prayer I spoke as a teenage boy standing on death's doorstep and the contemplative prayer that marks my current pattern are not the only ways I have addressed God in the times I set aside for my private devotions. There have been times when I have taken my confusion, fear, pain, or rage into the chapel with me. At those times my prayer has not begun with me sitting serenely in my prayer stall, letting the words that lead me into contemplation fall away. Many times my prayer has begun with tears. I have swept into my chapel to remonstrate with God, to fight with God. I have gone to God to pour out my anger or my despair. The marches that filled the streets of Cape Town in September 1989 and marked the beginning of the end of apartheid began that way.

In the weeks leading up to (what would be the last) apartheid Election Day, a coalition of antiapartheid civic and religious groups had led a campaign of civil disobedience. People of all races had joined in the antiapartheid action. But the vast majority of those protesting were people of color, poor people, or young people with little to lose. The government had responded, quite predictably, with brute force.

By that time I was a Nobel laureate. I was the archbishop of Cape Town and metropolitan of the Church of the Province of Southern Africa. News outlets around the world documented my steps and quoted my utterances. The South African police were masters of propaganda. They could imagine the consequences of news footage of me and other internationally recognized antiapartheid leaders being beaten and bloodied by baton-wielding officers. The pattern they established was to remove recognizable leaders from the scene and detain them for a few hours. Once the news magnets and the cameras were gone, they would baton-charge the remaining protesters.

In the central business district of Cape Town, where protestors were people of all races, the police used batons and water cannons on the activists. White protestors were stunned by the response. Few white South Africans had felt the wrath of the South African police. In the black and "colored" townships outside the city, the police reaction was lethal. They used live ammunition to disperse the crowds. On Election Day, Wednesday, September 6, 1989, the government-run

media reported that twenty people were killed in clashes between police and protesters. We planned to hold a memorial
service at St. George's Anglican Cathedral, in the center of
Cape Town, at lunchtime on Friday. On Thursday evening,
September 7, my assistant, Matt Esau, came to tell me that
reports on the ground put the death toll in the townships
that surrounded Cape Town much higher than twenty.
Shocked, angry, and in tears, I went to the chapel to pray.

During a sleepless, prayerful night I became convinced
that I must call for another march. Not I, but a "God-pressure"
in me.

I don't quite know how to describe "God-pressure."
There is a physical sensation, breathlessness, and a sense of
being weighed down by a heavy burden. But neither of those
is the main thing. The main thing is the sense of compulsion.
It is a loving compulsion. But "God-pressure" is a feeling of
being compelled to act, even against the voice of reason.

In calling for a march I was acting against reason and
logic. No calculation on my part would have inspired the
idea of a march. After all, we knew how other marches had
ended in violence and death. But I knew that in this I was not
my own master. I could not do otherwise. On Friday morning I told my staff that, at the midday memorial service, I
would call for a new protest to be held on Monday morning.
At the urging of Matt Esau, I agreed to delay the proposed
march by two days. God, I suppose, is not usually terribly
concerned with the details. The exact date and time did not
matter. All I knew was that the march had to happen. And
it had to happen soon. We made the announcement at the

memorial service that day. After the tiring, tense, and bloody weeks that had preceded the elections, we knew that people might be battle weary. We hoped that perhaps a thousand people would take to the streets the following Wednesday.

The response to our call was unprecedented. On Wednesday, September 13, 1989, a carnival of Capetonians, thirty thousand strong, surged down Adderley Street and around to the open square in front of city hall. People of every race, creed, class, and color joined the protest. Muslim imams linked arms with Jewish rabbis and Christian bishops. Smart straw-hatted girls from the best "white people only" private schools marched alongside black street sweepers. Lawyers and businessmen in natty suits followed a phalanx of tattily clothed boys from the township that danced a lively *toyi-toyi* down Cape Town's main street. Factory workers, dockworkers, politicians, and the unemployed joined the throng. This was the Rainbow Nation. We were united under a bright banner that read "Peace in our city: Stop the killings." Activists from the antiapartheid United Democratic Front served as marshals, because the police were nowhere in sight. In the wake of this march a wave of peaceful protests swept the country. They were not met with the brutality of previous civic actions. Something had changed.

One might be able to argue that the march was just a bright idea, nothing God-inspired. But it really ought not to have happened. For one thing, it should have been impossible to organize. Some of my colleagues took me to task for acting with no mandate from the antiapartheid organizations. But they came on board. I didn't know what the new mayor of Cape Town, Gordon Oliver, would do. He came to the memorial service on Friday. He decided then and there to join the march. For the first time in our history, a South African city granted official permission for a protest march.

When I called for the march I didn't know what was going on in the meeting rooms of the apartheid government. I did not know of the "palace coup" that had effectively side-lined the incumbent president, the racist and autocratic P. W Botha. I had no idea that the president-elect, F. W. de Klerk, had already, effectively, assumed the reigns of leadership. I certainly did not know that he was a different kind of man from his predecessor. De Klerk was a shrewd and sophisti-cated politician. I didn't know that he was making a differ-ent calculation. He wasn't trying to quash dissent in order to maintain a stranglehold on power. He had decided that the forces for and against apartheid had reached a stalemate. He was calculating how to orchestrate a transformation that would satisfy the black majority and secure the future of the white minority. I did not know any of that then. But God knew. And the march happened.

No one could have orchestrated the congruence of events, decisions, and people that made it all work. But, amazingly, it did all work. I acted on the insistent prodding of my own prayer, and the obstacles that seemed guaranteed to thwart our plans fell away. It may all have been a series of grand coincidences. But, as the Anglican archbishop William Temple observed, "When I pray, coincidences happen. When I don't, they don't."

Anyone's prayer can give rise to the coincidences that Archbishop Temple describes. Anyone might, at some time in her life, experience "God-pressure." Attending to that God-pressure will not necessarily mean that we bring thousands to the streets in a protest march or that we will face down a row of armored tanks like that lone protestor at Tiananmen Square. What God-pressure does mean for each and all of us is that, when we attend to it, we will live lives of flourishing that promote lives of flourishing.

Perhaps you have not experienced God-pressure in your own life. After all, it is not the only way that God communicates with us. Sometimes God speaks to us in the very words that we pray. In Mpho's home her family gathers for nightly prayers that begin with a recitation of what Christians call the Lord's Prayer:

Our Father, who art in heaven,
Hallowed be thy Name,
Thy kingdom come,
Thy will be done on earth as it is in heaven.
Give us this day our daily bread
And forgive us our trespasses,
As we forgive those who trespass against us.
And lead us not into temptation,
But deliver us from evil,
For thine is the kingdom,
And the power, and the glory,
Forever and ever. Amen.

On some nights, Mpho has confided, she just rattles her way through the prayer—perhaps, in a way, akin to people reciting the pledge of allegiance—but every so often, a word or a phrase or a portion of the prayer will "arrest" her attention: "Forgive us . . . as we forgive." "Do I really want to be the one who sets the standard for forgiveness?" she muses. "And what will happen if I am forgiven only as far as my own forgiveness reaches? If that is true, then what about that incident with my spouse for which I have not yet forgiven him? What will become of me and the many thoughts, words, and deeds for which I need forgiveness? Will I be forgiven for yelling at the kids? Will I be forgiven for thinking snide thoughts about the receptionist?" In the words of a familiar prayer God can speak to our logical minds. It is said that praying shapes believing. The creedal statements that are a part of so many faiths, the hymns, chants, and poems that are expressions of worship can also be ways that God chooses to address us. The familiar prayer spoken or sung with barely a thought may be the door that God uses to enter more fully into our consciousness.

Time, place, company, and mood will dictate how we address God. In like manner, God has a variety of ways to communicate with us. The door of opportunity that opens or closes unexpectedly can be God's way of turning our attention in a new direction. The inspired choice, the irresistible pressure, the word or idea that will not let us go are all ways that God talks to us. The prick of conscience, the comment of a friend or stranger that edges under our skin—these, too, are ways that God communicates with us. Human beings can be messengers of God. They can speak to us on God's behalf. In fact, the word *angel* comes from the Greek *angelos*. *Angelos* is a translation of the Hebrew *mal'ak*, "messenger." The Hebrew does not carry with it the connotation "dead person with wings"; it simply means "messenger." That messenger may be human or divine. The practice of prayer helps us to discern, from among the many voices we hear and choices we face each day, which is the guiding voice of God.

The challenge of distinguishing the voice of God from all the voices that vie for our attention is not unique to our time. Jesus used the metaphor of the shepherd to reassure his followers that they *can* recognize the voice of God from among the voices they hear. In Jesus's time, the sheep that belonged to the members of a village or community would be penned together overnight. In the morning each shepherd would come to the gate of the enclosure. He would call his sheep and lead them out to pasture. The sheep could distinguish among the voices of all the shepherds, and they would follow the sound of *their* shepherd's voice. Our times of prayer are the times when we learn the guiding voice of goodness, *our* shepherd's voice. In our daily lives, when the stillness has fled and the fullness of life has rushed back in on us, we will still be able to discern the voice that calls us to our best selves from among the many voices that compete for our attention.

The competition for our attention is fierce. The voices of our own desires claw at us. Inside our heads the voices of employers or workplace supervisors drone on with unsatisfied demands. On our internal play list, the voices of friends and family are an unending clamor. Our hopes, our joys, our rages, and our fears create a raucous crowd. But even in the midst of that riot there is a quiet, constant voice that guides us to goodness. The voice of God is an affirming voice. It does not reduce us or belittle us. It seeks to enhance life. It speaks on behalf of life. The voice of God speaks up on behalf of good. The practice of prayer attunes us to that voice.

Of course, as the practice of prayer helps to make us sensitive to the voice of goodness, there are habits that can make us tone-deaf to that voice. We can be like Adam and Eve, who chose to listen to the lures of the serpent and ignore the guidance of God. We can choose to let the noise of our wants and whims muffle the sound of God's voice. The seductions of money and power are very real. The voice of greed is like the mythological siren song, irresistible if we listen to it. The financial upheaval of recent years and the tales of corruption in so many parts of the world testify to that truth. The voice of greed is the voice of fear. We are afraid that there will not be enough for us, so we hoard. The money and things that we amass with such desperation become sound barriers. They muffle the voice of God.

The wisdom that goodness offers tells us that all of us can flourish. But the noisy demands of tribe and nation can drown out that voice of reason. So we spend obscene amounts of money on deadly defenses. We ignore the truth that a fraction of the world's military budgets would buy us genuine safety by ensuring adequate clean water, clothing, food, and shelter for every person on our planet. We engage in fierce arguments over who should be first to make real reductions in carbon emissions even though the environmental threat of catastrophic climate change looms over all of us. When we listen to the voices of greed, tribalism, and nationalism, when we feed our lust for power with the attention it craves, we become tone-deaf to the voice of God, who guides us toward goodness.

Our noisy passions are like an unruly kindergarten class. Each hope, fear, ambition, dream, and desire tries to shout louder than the others to make itself heard. The voice of God guides like a gifted teacher. The experienced teacher does not address the class with a booming voice to be heard above the din. He speaks quietly and calmly, a steady current beneath the noise. To this child a word and a touch, to this one a look and a murmur, until each child—curiosity piqued—hushes so he or she can listen. The calm and constant presence below the undisciplined tumult of our ideas and emotions is the voice of God guiding us to goodness.

We can continue to react to the insistent demands of our unruly passions and remain tone-deaf to God. Or we can use the practice of prayer to help us hear, ever more perfectly, the guidance that God offers. God is our constant companion. God can help us to choose, from among the plethora of paths that are spread out before us, the one that leads to flourishing. The guide who becomes known to us in prayer steadies us when we stumble and cradles us when we fall. That guide can show us the way back to goodness, however far from the path we stray.

Prayer is the time and place to hear God's guidance for our lives. Prayer is also where we are best able to hear the voice of God's loving acceptance. In the next chapter we will explore the gift of God's acceptance and learn what it means for our lives. I will begin by telling you about a time when I was reminded of this godly acceptance, which is perhaps best exemplified by a grandparent's doting love.

But first let us turn into the stillness and listen to God speak with the voice of the heart.

Child, do you not know my voice?
It bubbles up in happy laughter:
Listen to your children play.
It echoes in the songs of nature:
Stop and listen.
I speak as fresh rain on parched ground,
I speak as the summer breeze that caresses the long grass,
I speak as the gurgle of the river over the rocks,
I speak in the warm smiles of welcome,
I speak in the tender touch of comfort,
I speak in tears of joy,
I speak as unquenchable hope.
I speak in the voices of those who challenge you;
Mine are the words of the loving rebuke.
I speak in the voices of those who take pride in you;
Mine are the words of honest praise.
My voice is the happy hum in your heart
When you know you have done what is right.
My voice is the churning in your spirit
When temptation seems ready to overwhelm you.

My voice whispers "courage"
When the path you must choose seems too long or too hard.
It is I who say, "Be still a while,"
When the frenzy wants to overtake you.

Have you not heard me yet?
I am very near.
I breathe in your breath,
I pray in your prayer,
Have you not heard me yet?
Stop and see.
Look, listen.
Yes,
That is me.

11

SEEING WITH GOD'S EYES

I was sitting in Mpho's room in the maternity ward, gazing at the newborn Onalenna. I heard my older granddaughter before I saw her. Her nine-year-old feet came clattering along the hospital corridor. Her happy squeals filled the air. "I have a sister! I have a sister!" Nyaniso burst into her mother's room bubbling over with glee. She only had eyes for the tiny bundle sleeping cradled in my arms. I smiled because her joy was infectious. I smiled because the clatter of her feet as she ran to meet her new baby sister echoed my own race across the township when my son, Thamsanqa, was born. Her sister's delight made evident that another child had come into the world, loved without remainder before she had spoken her first word or taken her first tottering step.

Babies are born every minute. And I saw again, brought into
the incredible beauty of the mundane, what it was to be perfectly loved and accepted before the first choice was made.
The unearned, unmerited, unconditional love had become
the inheritance of another child. One more person inhaled
with her first breath the savor of God's love.

Even if no sister squealed her delight at your birth, even
if no parent ran to proclaim the joyful news, God's love preceded you into your life. You drew in God's acceptance with
your first breath. Accepting God's acceptance is what allows
us to live out of our own godliness. It is what helps us to live
into our own goodness.

It can be hard to take in God's acceptance, to assimilate it,
to feel it in our bones and own it. Even if we have had glimpses
of God's acceptance in the acceptance that the people who
love us can offer, we find it hard to hold on to the truth that,
for God, we have nothing to earn, nothing to prove. We are
accepted just as we are. Experiences of acceptance from the
people nearest to us can help us to trust God's acceptance.
The love we receive from the people dearest to us can help
us to trust God's love. The imperfect love of human beings is
patterned on the perfect love of God.

For children, especially for teenagers, it is often their
grandparents who animate the gift of acceptance. The teenage years are a time of testing. They are also a time when
children are desperate to know that someone in their world
finds them lovable no matter what. Grandparents can be
the embodiment of that unconditional acceptance. Perhaps
it is the grace of critical distance that makes this possible. I

know that my relationships with my own grandchildren are very different from the relationships I had with their parents. After all, it is not my duty to raise the grandchildren. All I have to do is love them and delight in them. And that is easy.

It is easy to be tickled by the antics of our grandchildren. I have not always trusted that it was easy to delight in me. But through the years I have been blessed with so many people who have "put skin on" God's love for me.

One person who showed me God's love "with skin on" was my maternal grandmother, Kuku, who brought me jam-filled treats at the end of the day. As was my mother, who made the long, weekly treks to the hospital when I was sick with tuberculosis. Before that, when at age six I had suffered a severe burn on my leg, she had made daily trips to that hospital to visit me. I hated that hospital too. I hated the food. I hated the smells. I hated being there. My mother had to have me discharged from the hospital early because my sustained piteous whimpering was disturbing the other pa-tients. Of course that meant more work for her, taking care of me at home.

Leah's love and acceptance have been sustenance through all these years of marriage. I don't have to imagine what acceptance feels like. I have experienced it. Having been given the gift of love "with skin on," I can offer it to others.

Even if there is no one in your life who has demonstrated the pattern of acceptance to you, it is a pattern that you can discover for yourself. It is a gift you can give yourself. You can come to recognize how beautiful you really are. You can come to know how precious you are to God. Do you have any idea how precious you are to God? Don't you know that you are so precious that even the hairs on your head are numbered? You are so precious that your name is inscribed on the palm of God's hand. It's not just written there—so that it might be erased, rubbed out. Your name is inscribed, etched, actually *carved* on the palm of God's hand.

I have met people who have discovered self-acceptance in the most unlikely circumstances. And when they discovered that self-acceptance, they found true peace. One young man who touched me deeply was Dominique Green. My friend Tom Cahill introduced him to me. When I met Dominique he was on death row awaiting execution. At the age of eighteen he had been arrested and charged with shooting a man during a robbery. Although he insisted that he had not been the gunman, an all-white jury in Texas convicted him. He spent the last twelve years of his life on death row.

He spent the first eighteen years of his life enmeshed in a different kind of horror. Dominique grew up in grinding poverty. His father was a drug dealer. His mother was an alcoholic and a prostitute. She was mentally deranged, a schizophrenic with multiple personalities. She abused her son. She would humiliate him verbally and brutalize him physically. If his behavior displeased her she would hold his right hand over an open flame to punish him. She beat him and tortured him, sometimes stubbing out her cigarettes in the palm of his hand.

He fled from home when his mother threatened to kill him. She had pointed a gun at him and pulled the trigger, by some miracle he was unhurt. He was fifteen years old. With his earnings from petty crime he rented a storage bin and made that his home. He had been living there for three years when he was arrested.

The young man I met had every right to be bitter, with a mean, shriveled heart. But he wasn't. In his twelve years in prison Dominique had blossomed into himself.

Dominique had become a writer and an editor. He compiled an anthology of inmates' writings. He had developed some expertise in the law. He helped fellow inmates with their legal briefs. He had become a voracious reader. After reading *No Future Without Forgiveness,* my book about South Africa's Truth and Reconciliation Commission, he decided that forgiveness was the path he must follow. He forgave all the people in his life who had wronged or failed him. Where possible he asked forgiveness from those he had harmed. He gave the book to his fellow death-row inmates and encouraged them to adopt forgiveness as the pattern for their own lives. Dominique was an inspiration. The widow of the man he had allegedly murdered and the children of the deceased campaigned for clemency in his case. In spite of international appeals, Dominique was executed on October 23, 2004.

Tied to the gurney while he waited for the lethal injection to take effect, Dominique told the witnesses, "I am not angry, but I am disappointed that I was denied justice." Dominique had decided not to live into the tormented meanness that he could claim as a birthright. He had chosen to live into the goodness that was his inheritance as a child of God. He had accepted the goodness that was the essence of Dominique. He had accepted himself.

The path to self-acceptance doesn't have to be as challenging as the one that Dominique traveled. The peace that is the fruit of self-acceptance is within every person's reach. Prayers and affirmations can mark the way. Meditation and mindfulness can help us to cultivate the habit of self-acceptance.

Cultivating the habit of self-acceptance allows us to live lives of wholeness. When we can accept our own frailties and limitations, we do not berate ourselves for what we cannot do, what is beyond the scope of our abilities. We learn to be at ease in our own bodies. We learn how to inhabit our own lives. When we recognize our own limitations, we can let go of the anxious quest for flawless lives.

Mpho often says she thinks that God sends us children to illustrate the difference between that anxious perfection that is flawlessness and the godly perfection that is wholeness. Living lives of wholeness is very possible for the parents of an infant. The baby's happy coos and chortles make adults' hearts sing. Flawlessness, on the other hand, is impossible. The happy cooing is quickly replaced by rancid spit-up and just as quickly reverts to happy cooing. Spit-up can put a quick kibosh on any notions of flawless perfection. Experienced mothers advise their inexperienced counterparts to let everything but the essentials slide in the early months of motherhood. The quest for flawlessness has no place in those exhausting weeks of recovery from childbirth when parents are discovering how to integrate a new, and demanding, person into the household. Of course dirty diapers, sleeplessness, and spit-up are not the only things that can teach us the difference between the comfortable perfection that is wholeness and the brittle perfection that is flawlessness.

The godly perfection that is wholeness and the very human experience of failure are not opposites. In fact, our failures may be the times when we are closest to God. This can be as true in our most intimate relationships as it is on the world stage. For instance, we are being faithful to our roles as parents when we speak the "no" of discipline that our children do not want to hear. Their defiance is a failure in the moment. But God is near us as we keep faith with our commitment to raise our children.

It may be the procession of faithful failures that enriches the soil of godly success. Faithful actions are not religious acts. They are not even necessarily actions undertaken by people of faith. Faithful actions, whether they are marked by success or they end in failure, are actions that are compelled by goodness.

In 1990 the National League for Democracy won 82 percent of the seats in the Burmese parliamentary elections. The leader of that party, Daw Aung San Suu Kyi, should have assumed the office of prime minister. Instead the military junta nullified the election results and placed Dr. Suu Kyi under house arrest. She was awarded the Nobel Peace Prize in 1991 but was not granted permission to travel to Oslo to claim that honor. Her sons, Alexander and Kim, went in her stead. She was released from house arrest in 1995, but the junta made it clear that if she left the country to visit her husband, British citizen Michael Aris, she would not be allowed to return. Her husband was diagnosed with prostate cancer in 1990. He was granted a visa to visit her in 1995. Subsequent visa requests were refused, and he died in 1999 without seeing her again. Her children live in England and are also refused permission to visit her.

Since 1990 she has endured repeated imprisonments and extended periods confined to her home under house arrest. She has been under house arrest since 2003, under an order of confinement that the military dictators renew each year. In 2009 an American eluded the security police who guard her. He swam across the lake to her home. Because of this, Suu Kyi stood trial for contravening the terms of her house arrest. The chief of the national police agreed that the American, John Yettaw, was the "main culprit" in the case. Despite this admission, on August 11, 2009, Suu Kyi, was sentenced to three years of imprisonment with hard labor. This sentence was commuted to an eighteen-month house arrest. This slight woman, buffeted by personal loss and national tragedy, continues to stand firm against the might of the military junta. "The only real prison is fear. The only real freedom is freedom from fear," she says.

Judging from the evidence of this moment in history, Daw Aung San Suu Kyi's every effort to bring peace, security, and democracy to her people has failed. It is the kind of failure that we in South Africa know all too well. Although in hindsight the end of apartheid was inevitable, there were times when the unbearable pain of the present veiled the shining hope for the future. It is almost two decades since the first multiracial elections. There is a generation that never knew the fierce grip of the apartheid machine. There are young people who do not remember pass laws, tear gas, or the "Free Mandela" campaign. Even those of us who lived through the dying days of apartheid cannot enumerate all the faithful failures that paved the road to our freedom.

So we can say with the confidence born of long experience that although Burma's democracy movement has failed for now, it is only for now. Even though Aung San Suu Kyi has failed in every attempt to overcome the military dictatorship, each failure has been a faithful failure. It has been failure born out of courage and goodness. Each failure has enriched the soil of eventual success. Because the end she seeks is flourishing for all her people, she has already succeeded. She has already won. What we used to say to the white government in the dark days of apartheid we say to the Burmese junta now: "Join the winning side. Sign up with the pro-democracy activists and join the winning side!"

The winning side is not only the province of politics. To join the winning side is to align ourselves with goodness. It is faithful action that each of us can practice in our own lives. We can choose to act out of the goodness that is the essence of our being. We do this not in a quest for success, that illusive target. Instead, in this as in all things, we can choose to seek godly perfection. Then it doesn't matter if we are successful in this moment, in our lifetime, or in our generation. It matters only that we are faithful.

We can choose goodness no matter the circumstances. We can always ask, "What is the answer my best self would give? What is the action my best self would take?" We can use that guidance to navigate the rocky shoals of an unhappy marriage. We can use it to traverse that broad desert of teen angst. We can use it to respond to a cruelty or to disappointment. We can use this guidance to help us choose what to take on and what to let go. When we stop being harried by the pursuit of success, our lives will reflect the goodness in us. And we will be able to recognize the goodness in others.

We will even be able to recognize the goodness in the people who hurt or anger us, those in need of our forgiveness. When we recognize the goodness hidden behind the harm they have caused, we will be able to forgive them and "re-member" them. We will be able to reclaim our common humanity, our membership in one family—the human family.

I know that forgiveness is hard work. Sometimes it may even feel like an impossible task. We cannot will it into being. We may be disposed to offer it but find our hearts as yet unready. Holding on to hurt and anger is burdensome. The pain of an insult takes up psychic space; it occupies territory that could be inhabited by joy.

Mpho offers people who participate in retreats with her a practice that can help to ease the way to forgiveness and freedom. She invites the members of her group to pick up a stone. It should be one with some heft and texture. But it should not be too large. It should be something that fits easily into the palm of the hand. For a whole day, keep that stone about your person. Tell the stone the whole story of the outrage, in as much detail as you can recall. Throughout the day, if you find your mind returning to the hurt, hold the stone and tell that stone your thoughts and feelings. At the end of the day, find a sacred space to set the stone down. You may want to place it in a churchyard, under a favorite tree, or near a river. As you set the stone down, set down the burden of hurt that you have been carrying. Know that the burden is in a safe place; you can reclaim it if you need it. But know also that you don't have to carry it. Laying down the burden of pain is one way of returning to goodness. It is a gift that we can give to ourselves rather than the answer to a commandment.

Just as the finger wagging "should" cannot sow forgiveness in our hearts, we cannot guilt ourselves into goodness. We can only guilt ourselves into "being good," which is not the same thing. "Being good" and "doing good" are not the same thing as the goodness, the wholeness we have been describing. Have you ever seen a film of a place that purports to be New York City though the movie was filmed in Toronto? The cities bear a passing resemblance to one another, but they are not the same thing. The goodness of which we speak bears a passing resemblance to "being good" or "doing good," but they are not the same thing. "Being good" and "doing good" are onerous duties. Goodness is all joy. It is not necessarily ease. It is not guaranteed happiness. But goodness is true joy.

The onerous duty of "doing good" disappears once we recognize that we have no need to impress God with our success. When we really grasp our own goodness, we realize that we have no need to "buy" God's approval. We are already loved. We are already accepted. When we can accept our acceptance, the texture of life changes. The fear that has held us hostage will release its stranglehold on us.

If we accept our own acceptance all of the things we hold to be inherent, negative attributes of human nature—greed and laziness, rage and jealousy—will be unmasked. We will come to recognize them as fear in disguise. We hoard against the fear that we will not have enough. We overspend because we think more things will silence our dread of having nothing. We are lazy and we procrastinate lest we prove to be incapable. We think that we can hide behind the fiction that we have not failed if we have not tried. We get enraged rather than admit that we are confused, hurt, worried, inadequate. So we yell angrily at the driver who cut us off rather than admit our genuine fear for our own safety and that of the children in the backseat.

The next time you are angry with your spouse or partner, ask yourself, "What am I afraid of?" Are you afraid that if he is right your power in the relationship will drain away? Are you afraid that if you are wrong you will be left alone? Are you afraid of being needed too much or of not being needed at all?

When we deny our fears or try to run from them, they loom over us, larger than life. When we can face our fears, they do not metastasize into something else. When we dare to name our fears, they shrink to a manageable size. If you can name your fear, you may recognize that same fear in others. Then, rather than create division, fear can open our eyes to our common humanity. That recognition can displace the jealousy that poisons so many relationships. We are jealous because we fear that if the other person is loved, applauded, or admired there will be no love, applause, or admiration left over for us. But there is enough for us. There is more than enough for all of us. There are enough of the material things in the world for us all to flourish. There are enough of the intangible things for all of us to thrive. But for us to engage in the practices that will ensure that we all prosper, we must come to know that each of us is linked in the chain of our common humanity. God dwells in each of us.

It is a radical claim. God dwells in each of us. God dwells in each of us even when we are unaware of it. It is radical not only in the sense that it is revolutionary. It is radical in that it is, literally, at the root of everything. And this is something that can't change, not even in the worst human being. The God who dwells in us is a part of us that cannot be destroyed. That is why we can never give up on anybody. It may explain why, for instance, when people have been pretty badly treated and you think that they are going to break, they do not. They recognize that they are made for more, for better than they have had to endure.

The kids in Soweto knew that they were made for something better than what they had endured. The children— and they were children, young teenagers, thirteen to sixteen years old—who organized the protest march in 1976 were brought up on Bantu Education. It was a system designed to destroy them. It was designed to make them into servants. It wanted to make them serfs who, in a sense, could not think for themselves, who were obsequious. But it was those kids who knew nothing better, in a sense, who stood up to the viciousness of the system. Why, when everything pointed to the fact that they should have succumbed? But they didn't succumb. They couldn't be cowed. God could not be miseducated out of them. They knew they were made for something more. They were certain that they were made for something better. Nothing could kill that certainty. Nothing could erase it. Nothing could destroy it.

God does dwell in us. This is the essential truth of who we are. We are creatures made in the image of God. At the core of our being is goodness. This is not to deny the reality of sin. Sin is real. Depravity and cruelty are real. Evil exists. But sin, cruelty, and evil are not our essential nature. They are aberrations. What is normative is goodness. Wrongness runs against the grain of creation. Evil is so contrary to our nature that we must construct justifications to allow ourselves to do what we know to be wrong or cruel. We concoct a justification or we claim that we are powerless to effect change. So we justify torture by saying that brutality might prevent widespread carnage. We avert our eyes from epidemic disease in poor countries, and we tolerate famine: "It's not that we don't care, we just didn't know it was so bad." Or "What are we supposed to do?" The justifications and the unease with our own inaction prove these behaviors to be anomalous. Goodness is our lodestone.

This was true for the girls I met at a school in Northern Ireland. They knew that goodness is the governing quality of humanity. They knew this despite what they had experienced. Cruelty and spite are not the essential qualities of human beings. They are departures from the human norm.

In November 2001, I visited Holy Cross School in Belfast. At that time relations between the Protestant and Roman Catholic communities were fraught. I asked to meet with the leaders of both sides at Stormont Castle, the headquarters of the Secretary of State for Northern Ireland. But each side would agree to meet with me only if representatives of the other side were not present. The hatred between the two groups was palpable. I had never before experienced anything like it.

I did meet with Gerry Adams, the president of Sinn Féin. I described him to my hosts, a protestant family who had lived and worked in South Africa. "I found him a warm and charming person," I reported. The parents received my observation with no comment. But one of the children— probably parroting a sentiment he'd heard expressed by the adults—responded, "He can't be charming. He's an evil man."

Children experience fear, just like adults. They have their own worries, and they adopt adult concerns. They sometimes take on adult opinions without the sophistication or the information to examine or challenge them. Like adults, they can have their vision obscured. The girls at Holy Cross School were different.

I had been invited to Holy Cross School because the children needed an armed escort to walk to school. I don't remember what had sparked the blockade of the school. But for five months the Roman Catholic girls who attended this elementary school had to run the gauntlet of very angry Protestant adults. The protestors were using the most vile and abusive language. They swore at the children. They assailed the youngsters by throwing urine-filled balloons at them.

When I went to the school I expected to find deeply traumatized, angry children. But these children were not acting out of the trauma playbook. The girls were like elementary school children anywhere. Even after the assaults of the morning they were in touch with the joy of being little girls. There was much nudging, giggling, and squirming. They had prepared a song for me. They sang "Make Me an Instrument of Your Peace." The adults suffered from an acute failure of vision. They could not see God in the little girls. The girls, on the other hand, were blessed with God-sight. They did not answer hate with hate. They could see beyond the unspeakably ugly behavior they faced to the essential goodness hidden behind the adults' fear.

Under our dehumanizing fear there is goodness. With patience and skill we can uncover it. It happened in South Africa. It happened in Northern Ireland too. The ugly fear and the raw hatred I saw in 2001 were in distinct contrast to the comity I experienced on a recent visit to Ireland. It seemed impossible that Martin McGuinness of the Roman Catholic Sinn Féin and his Protestant counterpart, Ian Paisley, would ever share a negotiating table. Yet I saw them share a joke. The image of those two men laughing together reminded me that even a failure of vision is not final. Because God always dwells in us—in all of us—there is always hope. There is always hope that the scales will fall from our eyes and we will see as God sees. Prayer makes the scales fall off faster.

In the last chapter we described prayer as a way of hearing God's voice. It is that. One gift of prayer is that in prayer we can hear the voice of God guiding and directing us. Another, equally important gift of prayer is that we can hear the voice of God accepting us. This, then, is the wonder. We are already loved and accepted. God knows us to be good. When we listen to the voice of God in prayer, we don't hear the carping of a dissatisfied parent who is constantly correcting us. We hear the voice of one who sees and loves the already of us. We hear the voice of one who knows and loves the not yet of our being. God loves who we are. God sees and loves who we are becoming. Prayer is also how we learn to see as God sees.

In our prayer we can begin to see ourselves as God sees us. We can begin to see ourselves as we truly are.

In God's vision, sin is not the essential and foundational truth about us. Goodness is. We are not originally sinners, distant from God. We are originally the crowning achievement of creation. We are those created in the image and likeness of God. We are created out of the abundance of God's love. We are created for God's joy. And we have choices. The choices we make sometimes lead us away from God. They lead us into sin. For Christians, finding our way home to God is not a "self-help" project. Jesus Christ is our hope for complete wholeness, for healing that is salvation. And that hope has already been accomplished. So we are constantly called to experience the truth about us: that we are beloved of God.

Sometimes it can be hard to see ourselves as God sees us. It can be impossible to imagine God's loving gaze. Maybe you don't recall ever being looked at lovingly. Perhaps you experience every gaze as critical, judgmental, disapproving, or, at best, indifferent. But that is not how God looks at us. God's gaze is like the gaze between lovers wrapped in a tender embrace. God looks at us the way a mother looks lovingly at her newborn baby. If you can see the loving gaze between mother and child in your mind's eye, you can begin a small meditation on being held in God's loving gaze. Once you are able to fix the gaze in your mind, put yourself in the sight line of the one gazing. Allow yourself to be the subject of that long, loving look. In this way you can imagine, then experience, the loving gaze that God turns to us. As we allow ourselves to accept God's acceptance, we can begin to accept our own goodness and beauty. With each glimpse of our own beauty we can begin to see the goodness and beauty in others.

Why does this seeing matter? What difference does it make? It makes all the difference in the world. How would it be to turn with God's loving gaze and see those we name as enemies? How would we treat them? What of the people we love so imperfectly? If we could see as God sees, what would we see? Would we see anyone who should fall outside the reach of our care? The pimps, prostitutes, and prisoners, the drug-dealers and the deranged, the illegal immigrants, the terrorists, the race baiters, the homophobes and haters— all are held in God's loving gaze. God's love overshadows us all. That drug addict on skid row, that street person smelling to high heaven—if we really had the eyes to see, they would give us a glimpse of God. God camouflages the divine glory, which would be blinding. But if we truly look, we can see.

With God's eyes we see our enemies as they are—a bundle of incomprehensible hurts and hatreds, anger sheathed in human form. And we see them as they truly are—people made in God's own image, with hopes, loves, laughter, blood, and tears like ours. With God's eyes we see our children as they are—a pimply jumble of faults and failings, forgotten homework and skipped chores. And we see them as they truly are—gifts to us of grace and wonder, treasurers of divine imagination, teachers who point us to God. With God's eyes we can see ourselves as we are, with all of our pride, every lack, all our limitations, and each prejudice. And we can see ourselves as we truly are—not sinners in need of saving but saints in need of seeing. And all of us are good. No, not just good, but very good. We are precious to God, the crown of creation, beautiful beyond compare. Very, very good.

Let us turn into the stillness and listen to God speak with the voice of the heart:

You are my child,
My beloved.
With you I am well pleased.
Stand beside me and see yourself,
Borrow my eyes so you can see perfectly.
When you look with my eyes then you will see
That the wrong you have done and the good left undone,
The words you have said that should not have been spoken,
The words you should have spoken but left unsaid,
The hurts you have caused,
The help you've not given
Are not the whole of the story of you.
You are not defined by what you did not achieve.
Your worth is not determined by success.
You were priceless before you drew your first breath,
Beautiful before dress or artifice,
Good at the core.

And now is time for unveiling
The goodness that is hidden behind the fear of failing.
You shout down your impulse to kindness in case it is shunned,
You suck in your smile,
You smother your laughter,
You hold back the hand that would help.
You crush your indignation

When you see people wronged or in pain
In case all you can do is not enough,
In case you cannot fix the fault,
In case you cannot soothe the searing,
In case you cannot make it right.
What does it matter if you do not make it right?
What does it matter if your efforts move no mountains?
It matters not at all.
It only matters that you live the truth of you.
It only matters that you push back the veil to let your goodness shine
    through.
It only matters that you live as I have made you.
It only matters that you are made for me,
Made like me,
Made for goodness.

ACKNOWLEDGMENTS

*S*i *swele imilomo."* We do not have mouths enough.

    We do not have mouths enough to utter all the thanks we want to say. So we will do the best we can with the mouths and the words we have.

We thank God for the skill and sensitivity of Doug Abrams, who is not only our editor but also a writing coach in disguise. We owe him a debt of gratitude for his many readings of this manuscript; for the gentle wisdom that has helped us to create a better "best" than we started out with. Thank you, Doug, for the all of the tweaking and polishing that has burnished our words. We thank you for helping us to bring this work to fruition. More than that, we thank you for your friendship, your self-giving, your goodness.

We thank God for the brilliant Lynn Franklin, our agent and our favorite visionary, who over the many years of our association has become family.

We are thankful for Mark Tauber at HarperOne, who had the original vision for this project and has given our work his consistent support, and for Mickey Maudlin, our exceptional editor, who offered the editorial insights that helped us shape our writing and who exercised his speed-reading skills to get this manuscript ready on deadline.

We are thankful too for Mary Clemmey, our British agent, who so champions our work, and for Judith Kendra, our dedicated publisher at Rider/Random House UK.

We are particularly grateful for our friends at the Fetzer Institute who let us have the retreat center to ourselves so Mpho and I could have time to think, talk, and pray (and I to play with my grandchildren) at the beginning of this project.

Mpho adds her warm thanks to her God-sister, Cassandra Goad, and Cassandra's husband, Erik Wetter Sanchez, and their children, who gave Mpho and her girls the run of South Park and the keys to the car for a whole month of writing time.

Thank you to Mpho's godfather, Martin Kenyon, for a fabulous respite in Wentnor and for his close reading and editing of the text halfway along.

Another thank you to Karen Moore of the Richmond Hill Community for reserving Mpho's special room in Richmond, and for opening her Hot Springs, North Carolina, home to Mpho and her family so Mpho could have time to write and rest.

I thank my staff at Mpilo Ministries and my colleagues at the Desmond Tutu Peace Foundation.

Mpho adds heartfelt thanks to Nicole Preston Luke for managing to keep her in a state of near sanity through this process, and for being willing to go above and beyond the call of duty, friendship, or even sisterhood. She also thanks Diane Byrne for all the artistry and thoroughness with which she has managed the additional workload at the Tutu Institute for Prayer & Pilgrimage in Mpho's near absence.

There is a special place in heaven for all the people who have cared for my grandchildren. Thank you Senora Maggie Prieto for all your years of kindness and love; thank you, "Miss M'ria," aka Maria Quinn, for a whole summer of fun and care; thank you again to our friends at the Fetzer Institute for recognizing that a place to be was not enough, that we needed the children to be cared for in the best possible way. It was done.

Mpho and I thank our family and our friends for all they have done to bring us to this book.

Joe, Nyaniso, and Onalenna are due special thanks for keeping the home fires burning while Mpho was hidden behind her computer. The girls are due kudos for taking their mommy out to hunt for rainbows, splash in puddles, try the "jumpy-jumpy," and catch wishes. Mpho thanks Joe for being a solid rock to lean on, a cushion against hurts, and a fount of wisdom.

My thanks go to Leah, Roro, for all these years of love and wisdom.

Mpho, as is often the case, gets the last word. *To Nomalizo, mummy, mama: thank you for teaching me how to be a woman and a mother and to you and daddy for teaching me how to be a priest. Thank you, daddy, for all the hours, all the edits, and for letting me do this with you.*